**GOOD NEWS
FOR
RICH AND POOR**

GOOD NEWS FOR RICH AND POOR

CHRISTIAN APPROACHES TO A NEW ECONOMIC ORDER

BY HARVEY SEIFERT

A DOING THE WORD
STUDY/ACTION RESOURCE
UNITED CHURCH PRESS • PHILADELPHIA

Copyright © 1976 by the United Church Press. Printed in the United States of America. All rights to this book are reserved. No part of the text or illustrations may be reproduced in any form without written permission of the publishers, except brief quotations used in connection with reviews in magazines or newspapers.

Good News for Rich and Poor was prepared as a resource for Doing the Word, one of the educational approaches of the Christian Education: Shared Approaches project initiated through the Joint Educational Development process. This resource has been prepared especially for use in the following denominations: Christian Church (Disciples of Christ), Church of the Brethren, Cumberland Presbyterian Church, Episcopal Church, Evangelical Covenant Church, Moravian Church, Presbyterian Church in Canada, Presbyterian Church in the United States, Reformed Church in America, United Church of Canada, United Church of Christ, United Methodist Church, United Presbyterian Church in the USA.

Library of Congress Cataloging in Publication Data

Seifert, Harvey.
  Good news for rich and poor.
  (A Doing the word study/action resource)
  Bibliography: p.
  1. Christianity and economics. I. Title.
BR115.E3S38   261.8   76-40211
ISBN 0-8298-0324-6

Scripture quotations, unless otherwise indicated, are from the *Revised Standard Version of the Bible,* copyrighted 1946 and 1952 by the Division of Christian Education, National Council of Churches, and are used by permission. Quotations from *The New English Bible* are © The Delegates of the Oxford University Press and the Syndics of the Cambridge University Press 1961 and 1970. Reprinted by permission. Chart 1, The Development Gap, p. 26, and Chart 3, 1974 Assistance as Percentage of GNP, p. 64, are from Arthur Simon, *Bread for the World* (Paramus, N.J.: Paulist Press, 1975), pp. 44 and 115 respectively. They are used by permission of Paulist Press. Chart 4, Comparison of U.S. Official Development Assistance and Selected U.S. Personal Consumption Expenditures, 1973, p. 75, is from *The U.S. and World Development: Agenda for Action, 1975* by James W. Howe, staff of the Overseas Development Council. © 1975 by the Overseas Development Council; excerpted and reprinted by permission of Praeger Publishers, Inc., New York. The table on p. 25 is from an article by Benjamin Okner, "Middle Class Tax Reform?" which appeared in *transaction,* March-April 1971 and is used by permission. The litany on pp. 95-99 was developed by Ewald J. Bash and Charles P. Lutz for the world hunger program of The American Lutheran Church, used by permission.

CONTENTS

PREFACE BY DIETER T. HESSEL	9
CHAPTER 1 THE NECESSITY OF NOVELTY	11
CHAPTER 2 INVITATIONS TO INNOVATION	23
CHAPTER 3 UNACCEPTABLE MODELS FOR CHANGE	36
CHAPTER 4 THE CONTOURS OF A NEW ORDER	47
CHAPTER 5 A NEW ECONOMY FOR THE WORLD	58
CHAPTER 6 CONSTRUCTIVE ACTION BY CHRISTIANS	71
SESSION PLANS	84
APPENDIX: A HUNGER LITANY IN THREE "LANGUAGES"	95
NOTES	100
ADDITIONAL READING	103

ILLUSTRATIONS

CARTOON FROM "BREAD FOR THE WORLD"	17
THE DEVELOPMENT GAP	26
CONTEMPORARY ALTERNATIVES	40
1974 ASSISTANCE AS PERCENTAGE OF GNP	64
COMPARISON OF U.S. OFFICIAL DEVELOPMENT ASSISTANCE AND SELECTED U.S. PERSONAL CONSUMPTION EXPENDITURES, 1973	75

PREFACE

At first glance the title of this study/action book may lack credibility. Does a new economic order promise anything but bad news to those who already live in relative affluence? "Good News for *Rich* and Poor" strikes many persons as nonsense. They assume that we are in a win-lose (or zero-sum) game, a tug-of-war over scarce resources, in which the poor have much to gain but the rich stand only to lose. They doubt that new economic policies could bring important gains to all people. They fail to see that the old order is a no-win situation described in the pithy warning of Habakkuk 2:8, NEB: "Because you yourself have plundered many nations, all the rest of the world will plunder you."

This book means what the title says. A new economic order can be welcome news for the rich as well as for the poor. Both rich and poor have a great deal to gain from a shift in economic priorities to a new range of heretofore neglected values and services. That is the kind of double-win possibility toward which Christian insight points. The gains of a new economic order, however, will also be accompanied by painful adjustments in both rich and poor countries. Nobody can avoid personal sacrifices, except those who have virtually nothing to sacrifice.

Harvey Seifert is well qualified by decades of teaching Christian ethics and exploring economic problems to write on this subject. He begins where Christians should—with a biblical-theological perspective on social change. The Bible witnesses to the out-of-bondage-bringing God who acts to bring in a new order with justice. The new order requires the rich to respond to the just claims of the poor, and emboldens rich and poor alike to work for human fulfillment through the enlargement of political liberty and economic opportunity.

How does that vision relate to the current world situation? Our economic success has occurred at the expense of an increasing number of poor people. All the transfer of technology, all the massive private investment, all the spiraling gross national products, all the military and economic aid have not yielded general affluence. On the contrary, these policies have widened the gap between rich and poor everywhere. Humanity is divided against itself. Our economic system shows deeply-rooted defects that must be corrected not by embracing such unacceptable alternatives as Communism or Fascism, but by working toward a better order. The last half of this book outlines a new economic order, suggests priorities for government and personal action, and underscores opportunities for constructive Christian response.

Christians in North America have a special chance to make a difference for economic justice by fostering new attitudes, lifestyles, and public policies—by becoming a constituency that does the Word in solidarity with the rest of the world. We are called to become more aware of economic issues at home and abroad, to comprehend and analyze the underlying causes, to act in support of government initiatives for change, and to reflect theologically on the effort.*

Professor Seifert urges us *not* to leave economic problems to the experts. (How do you suppose we got our current difficulties?) In mistaken humility we have surrendered to special interest groups the power to define or decide questions of life and death that lie behind every technical argument. We who have experienced the righteousness of God and affirm the biblical vision of love and justice cannot responsibly refuse the call to support the dignity and rights of all persons, as well as to seek a fair distribution and sound use of the earth's resources for the benefit of life everywhere.

      Dieter T. Hessel
      Program Agency
      United Presbyterian Church in the USA

---

*An explanation of the ecumenical social education approach for which this resource was commissioned appears in the session plans at the back of the book.

CHAPTER 1
THE NECESSITY OF NOVELTY

A magazine cartoon showed several prosperous businessmen conferring with their chief. The harried-looking head of the firm was shouting into the intercom, "Miss Dugan, will you send someone in here who can distinguish right from wrong?" Instead of business executives, the conferees might just as well have been labor leaders, university trustees, city council-persons, or even delegates to a church convention.

Not only are there perplexing questions popping up all over the map, but some of the most popular proposals for solutions could result in wiping humankind off the globe. It is hard these days to sort out the right answer from the confused clamor of conflicting claims. Brazilian archbishop Dom Helder Camara insists, "The economic and cultural structures that dominate the world are suppressing more than two-thirds of humanity. They are killing and destroying more people than the bloodiest of wars."[1] The president of Algeria charges that the United States and Europe have plundered the natural wealth of the long list of poorer nations often called the Third and Fourth Worlds* (the developed capitalist and communist nations being the First and Second Worlds). He adds that whatever contributions the industrialized nations make should be considered "a simple restitution of a tiny part of the debt contracted by their odious exploitation."[2] At the same time a western diplomat was insisting, "It isn't totally our fault that some of them are poor. Some of them were just lazy."[3]

In the United States, "welfare rights" people are demanding the end of involuntary poverty in our land. At the same time others advocate harsher measures against those they call "welfare chiselers." Some find the cause of our economic woes in government regulation. Others see no cure apart from more government regulation. The world's newspapers report street brawls and revolutionary movements.

*Until recently, "Third World" meant all the developing countries. Some of them are faced with such poverty (e.g., Bangladesh, sub-Saharan Africa, parts of Latin America) that they are being called the "Fourth World."

Capitalists square off against Socialists, and Communists against Fascists. Large segments of youth, organized labor, and the business community are demanding drastic changes. Everybody wants "justice," but when they start to describe it, different speakers begin to contradict each other.

All of this seems confusing and discouraging. Yet anyone with an alert historical sense can find this tremendously exhilarating and encouraging. Sweeping improvements are never made without a time of troubles. It is out of confusion and conflict that vastly superior arrangements of economic and social life may emerge. When many things are simultaneously to be set right side up, a lot of things are turned over. The Hebrews would never have made it to the "promised land" had they not slogged through the dangers and difficulties of the wilderness.

This generation may add another chapter to history even greater than the emancipation of slaves, the winning of labor's right to organize, the establishment of social security protections, or legal guarantees of civil rights for ethnic minorities. We may accomplish the equivalent of the Protestant Reformation, Industrial Revolution, and birth of democracy—perhaps all rolled into one. All such changes come with turmoil and conflict. Even so, alert persons will heartily echo the words of Ralph Waldo Emerson:

> If there is any period one would desire to be born in—is it not the era of revolution when the old and the new stand side by side and admit of being compared; when all the energies of humankind are searched by fear and hope; when the historic glories of the old can be compensated by the rich possibilities of the new era?

CHANGE AND THE CHRISTIAN HERITAGE

Of all people, Christians should best understand current demands for something new and better. We may or may not agree with a particular program that is being proposed, but we can understand the need for continuous improvement. Precisely because we take seriously the lessons of history and the traditions of our faith, we, too, press for positive changes.

The pages of the Bible are enriched with visions of transformation. There are references to an in-breaking kingdom, a new wine, a new song, a new creature in Christ, a new commandment of love, and (in an all-inclusive sweep) a new heaven and a new earth. After recounting mighty works of God in the past, Isaiah interprets the word of the Lord, "Cease to dwell on days gone by and to brood over past history. Here and now I will do a new thing; this moment it will break from the bud.

Can you not perceive it? I will make a way even through the wilderness, and paths in the barren desert" (Isa. 43:18-19, NEB). The new revelation in Christ was expressed in his repeated words, "You have heard that it was said to the men of old. . . . But I say to you . . ." (Matt. 5:21-22, 27-28, 33-34, 38-39, 43-44). The book of Revelation puts it in the triumphant summation, "Behold, I make all things new" (Rev. 21:5).

No other conclusion is possible if one believes in a God whose perfection exceeds any present attainment of even the noblest persons, and whose love desires the best for all humankind. No matter where we stand, God always calls us forward. *Every*thing that persons and institutions do is to be improved. God always supports creative transformation.

Not only did God in the long distant past lay the foundations of the world. God also continues creative activity toward liberating the highest potentialities in nature and persons. The world and its people are still in the making. A Latin American theologian, Rubem Alves, wrote, "In the Biblical world, *one hopes for the future because one has already seen the creative event taking place in the past.*"[4] In the same book Alves has a chapter entitled "The Abortion of the Creative Possibility," in which he warns that creativity dies when we accept the illusion that existing reality is what we dream and hope for.

Another basic article in the Christian faith is that, along with their capacities for evil, persons have great unrealized potentialities for good. "We are God's children now; it does not yet appear what we shall be" (1 John 3:2). Paul might speak for each of us when he said, "When I was a child, I spoke like a child, I thought like a child . . .; when I became a man, I gave up childish ways." The mature life involves the fullness of faith, hope and love, with "the greatest of these" being love (1 Cor. 13:11-13). We obstruct God's intention when we prolong our own adolescence. Since we have not attained spiritual adulthood, we continuously "press on toward the goal for the prize of the upward call of God in Christ Jesus" (Phil. 3:14).

The significance of life is to be found in this change process. Our love is always imperfect and partially unrealized. There is unending need for "conscientization," or the birth of a new consciousness through awareness, analysis, action, and reflection. There are open horizons for exploration, untapped resources for creativity. New expressions of love inevitably grow out of genuine sensitivity to emerging needs. When loving persons realize what life is like for the poor, or for minority ethnic groups, or for those in the developing world, they are driven by the anguish of sympathetic identification to recognize their own responsibility. We may try to save ourselves from pain by becoming rigid and insensitive. But this is a fool's paradise. It is like shutting off the radar that shows an iceberg bearing down on our ship, rather than changing course.

In the light of basic Christian insights, social change is *always* to be expected, and constructive change is always to be supported. The consequences for our attitudes and actions may come as a jolting shock, because they are so often overlooked and unexpected.

1. It is impossible to relate intimately to God unless we join God in working for the dispossessed of the earth. If we want to stand close to God, we must also stand close to the poor, the oppressed, and the helpless. With the poor is where God stands.

Amos described God as not listening to the worship of the people because they perpetrated injustice (Amos 5:21-24). His words might be given a modern paraphrase by having God say, "I hate, I despise your Sunday services, even though you bring huge offerings and partake of many sacraments. Take away from me the noise of your hymns and choir anthems. But let justice roll down like waters, and righteousness like an everflowing stream." Comparable words of Jesus were, "If you are offering your gift at the altar, and there remember that your brother has something against you, leave your gift there before the altar and go; first be reconciled to your brother, and then come and offer your gift" (Matt. 5:23-24).

These days when many of our brothers and sisters have a great deal against us, if we took the words of Jesus literally there would be a mass rush from sanctuaries into a variety of action projects. Social action is a prerequisite to genuine worship, just as sincere worship is a stimulator for social action.

2. If we believe at every point what we believed even ten years ago, we have not taken the Christian faith seriously enough. Of course, we will continue to believe a great deal far longer than a decade, because some of our views are reasonably sound and no better insight comes to us. At the same time we know that all of our opinions are tainted with human finitude, and that we do not yet fully understand the meaning of Jesus or the truth of God. Everything that any person thinks or does can be improved. There is no improvement without change, and there is no change without leaving one's old position. To be a Christian is to grow continuously. Jesus was vigorously opposed to self-satisfaction, and to the pride which this indicates (Luke 18:9-14). Repentance and an enlarged dedication are always in order (Matthew 5:17; Luke 13:1-5). Whenever *all* our attitudes, opinions, and actions remain the same for a considerable period, we have given up the Christian quest.

3. In the light of God's intention, the burden of proof is always on

the status quo, both personally and socially. God wants more for persons than any social situation is providing. The good news of the gospel is always new news, the announcement of what has never been realized before. Any existing human arrangement is always put on the defensive. Many aspects may be preserved as the best we have yet been able to devise. Yet, from the Christian perspective, every existing political and economic order is at least partially obsolete. To accept the word of God is to refuse to accept present social structures and practices in their entirety.

4. Anyone aware of this dimension of the Christian faith cannot be a consistent conservative. That is, he or she cannot believe that we should preserve everything as it now exists. At numerous points of serious imperfection, such a person must advocate change of either a milder liberal nature or of a more thoroughgoing radical kind. We cannot move into a more promising future without recognizing that there is something better available than present arrangements.

5. Only those who receive serious opposition from some groups are likely to be standing for much significant transformation. Those who are content with, or profit by, existing situations are not likely to accept kindly any strenuous proposals for change.

Throughout history, deeply dedicated Christians have had to accept the suffering that always accompanies serious nonconformity—along with the ecstasy of acceptance by God. The emphasis of Jesus was, "Blessed are you when men revile you and persecute you and utter all kinds of evil against you falsely on my account. Rejoice and be glad . . ." (Matt. 5:11-12). 1 Peter (4:12-14) also speaks of the normalcy of opposition. "Do not be surprised at the fiery ordeal which comes upon you to prove you, as though something strange were happening to you. But rejoice in so far as you share Christ's sufferings. . . . If you are reproached for the name of Christ, you are blessed, because the spirit of glory and of God rests upon you."

6. Newness is not threat but rather opportunity. Because we feel more comfortable with established habits and familiar situations, we feel threatened by proposals for change. But such comfort is shallow and short-lived. When we face the prospect of global hunger, nuclear war, worldwide revolution, and environmental exhaustion, the immediate discomforts of constructive change are far outweighed by long-run benefits.

The great prerequisite of social and spiritual growth is openness to the new. Growth through prayer and meditation requires a willingness to lay aside our existing prejudices and habits before we can receive a more satisfying word from God. Success in business and progress in the nation depend on the willingness to adapt to new circumstances by substituting new patterns for old. Valid proposals that are also novel are to be grabbed with both hands as gifts from God.

CRITERIA FOR CHANGE

Criteria for judging the validity of social proposals are also provided by the Christian faith. The Bible, corroborated by historical experience, defines direction for change. Christian ethical goals involve liberation and nurture of the highest capacities of every person on earth. That is what the norm of love means. The scope of Christian love is limited by no boundaries. It includes even enemies (Matthew 5:43-48). If we could imagine a gigantic telephone directory or computer printout listing every person in this and future generations, we could put a finger down on any page at random, and the person pointed to would deserve the fullest service we can possibly provide.

The relationship of love involves an intimate, supportive community. Instead of being characterized by schisms, wars, or exploitation, society would become inclusive, peaceful, and cooperative. The Christian is always interested in beating swords into plowshares, in breaking down walls and replacing them with communication lines. This also means that individual interests are to be subordinated to the common good. Instead of asking primarily what society can do for me, the more important question is what I can do for society. It is more accurate to say "What is good for the country is good for General Motors (or the auto workers' union)," than it is to say, "What is good for General Motors (or the UAW) is good for the country."

One important value we seek for the most possible persons is access to those material goods that are helpful to their highest development. There are higher values than material things, but material essentials are prior values. We must maintain life to have any other experiences. Economic essentials are necessary means toward even more important ends. Biblical writers delighted in the enjoyment of food and in the other gifts of God's physical creation. Jesus enjoyed banquets and was always sensitive to physical needs.

Ours is not a world-renouncing religion. We are not called to be ascetics, in the sense of shunning all material goods because we consider them to be evil. We are called to prevent material resources being used in evil ways. Too great an accumulation by a few may rob others. In terms of important aids to abundant life, God wants each human being to travel as close to first class as possible. Insofar as we shut up any group of persons in steerage with inadequate food or possessions, we are engaged in a devilish activity.

The requirement of justice has often been described as "to each his due." From the Christian perspective, that which is due to each is the fullest possible measure of all those things that contribute to actualization of the highest human potentialities. This is the purpose of God's creation. The earth and its resources belong to God (Leviticus 25:23; Psalm 24:1). We are simply stewards, managing these resources for God's purposes. Our guideline becomes equal opportunity for all. A basic principle of justice is to treat every person's inherent claim equally. Every child is to be given the maximum possible opportunity for the best which life has to offer. Failure to work for this possibility is as serious as infanticide.

This does not necessarily mean equal distribution of wealth. As a matter of fact, equal opportunity would require some inequality. When one has had long sieges of illness, for example, that person has the same opportunity only if he or she has more assistance in meeting medical expenses. But differences in need would not justify nearly the inequalities in wealth that now exist. An important way to evaluate any society is to see what happens to the least fortunate or the most disadvantaged of its citizens. Whenever, through no fault of their own, some starve while others grow fat, something is very seriously wrong. We would condemn a doctor who took better care of rich than of poor patients. Yet as a society we do just that.

Vadillo—Ovaciones, Mexico

The biblical view leaps beyond our usual notions about distributive justice. If a biblically-sanctioned program were proposed to Congress, it would be considered too radical to adopt. For one thing, it would go much further in emphasizing the legitimate claim that the poor have on society as a whole. Proverbs (14:31) insisted, "He who oppresses a poor man insults his Maker." God "does not forget the cry of the afflicted" (Ps. 9:12). Like a refrain throughout the Bible, God is seen as providing for the needs of the poor. (For example, see Psalms 12:5; 132:15; Isaiah 25:4; 41:17; 2 Corinthians 9:9.) To us likewise it is said, "Open wide your hand to your brother, to the needy and to the poor" (Deut. 15:11). It was considered a mark of righteousness when one could say, "I was a father to the poor, and I searched out the cause of him whom I did not know. I broke the fangs of the unrighteous, and made him drop his prey from his teeth" (Job 29:16-17).

Under the Deuteronomic code, the poor were allowed to glean anything left behind in fields and vineyards. Owners were not to be too thorough in the harvest, in order that some would be left for the poor (Deuteronomy 24:19-22; Leviticus 19:9-10; 23:22). The prophets repeatedly defended the rights of the poor.

Jesus described his ministry as to the poor and needy (Luke 4:16-19). For his association with the outcasts and the needy he was willing to confront the criticisms of the power structure (Matthew 11:19; Luke 7:34). To illustrate the relationship of love he told the parable of the good Samaritan (Luke 10:29-37). The ethical message of the parable might be summarized as saying that need anywhere constitutes a claim on resources everywhere. The existence of need alone is enough to release the action of love. Again, in the picture of the great judgment, action in response to need is the basis for entering into the presence of God (Matthew 25:31-46). We might well reread this, remembering that "When did we see thee hungry?" has special meaning in this day of world famine.

A *second* proposition from the Bible, which conspicuously challenges present attitudes and customs, is that the poor have a just claim particularly on the rich and the powerful. (While reading this next section, keep in mind that in comparison with most of the rest of the world we are fantastically wealthy.) While the Bible saw values in material things, it took a negative view of the possession of great wealth while there were those who were poor. Those who "covet fields, and seize them" thereby "oppress a man and his house" (Mic. 2:2). The prophets sternly condemned those who "trample upon the poor" (Amos 2:6-7; 5:11-12; 6:1, 3-6; Isaiah 3:14-15; 58:1-7). Those with unjust wealth are like hunters setting traps for human beings (Jeremiah 5:26-28). Religious laws were designed to protect the poor from the rich by what would sometimes seem to us drastic measures. Money is to be lent to the poor without charging interest. Debts are to be remitted every seventh year (Exodus 22:25-27; Deuteronomy 15:1-2; Leviticus 25:25-28, 35-41). The privileged have greater responsibility for equitable distribution because they have more resources (Luke 12:48).

The responsibility of the rich goes beyond voluntary or optional generosity. The very existence of the poor constitutes an inescapable claim on wealth (Deuteronomy 15:7-8). The responsibility of the poor includes hard work and self-help, but they are entitled to the protections of a more just and humane social order.

It is serious sin for the rich to harden their hearts toward the poor. This alienates the wealthy from God and blocks their own spiritual growth. Riches easily become an impediment to salvation. Jesus said, "Woe to you that are rich" and, in the parable of the wealthy farmer, labeled the rich man as "fool" (Luke 6:24-26; 12:16-21). As in the parable of the rich man and poor Lazarus, the great reversal of the coming reign of God will place the poor and powerless ahead of the apathetic rich and powerful (Luke 16:19-31). In the parable of the soils, "delight in riches" is one of the thorns that choke out the seed (Mark 4:19). Such a person "remains in death" because he or she does not love "in deed and in truth." "If any one has the world's goods and sees his brother in need, yet closes his heart against him, how does God's love abide in him?" (1 John 3:14, 17-18).

Accumulation of wealth easily becomes a goal opposed to devotion to God; thus one cannot serve both "God and mammon" (Matthew 6:24-25; Luke 16:13). "It is easier for a camel to go through the eye of a needle than for a rich man to enter the kingdom of God" (Matt. 19:24; Mark 10:25). As Helmut Gollwitzer pointed out, when affluent nations insist on continuously raising their own standards of living, they doom their own souls along with the lives of starving masses.[5] Ours is a theological crisis, a spiritual problem. Americans need to stress an ethics for the affluent, because we are the rich facing the eye of a needle.

Jesus, of course, related also to the rich. They also have needs to be met. They too are to be loved. But with respect to material goods, service to the rich is helping them give priority to the poor in their stewardship of wealth. Even the church too easily forgets this and falls under the condemnation of James 2:1-7, 14-17, 26. It is hard for disproportionately prosperous persons to hear this part of the word of God. As modern liberation theologians point out, we have a great deal to learn from those who know from experience what poverty is. These theologians insist that industrialized nations can hear the full word of

God only if they have an Easter experience, dying to their present limited values and being reborn with sensitivity to the poor of the world. Theologians from the Third and Fourth Worlds often insist that in striving for economic justice for the poor they are also contributing to the spiritual salvation of the rich.[6] Before we react to that defensively and self-righteously, we had better spend some time with our Bibles and in prayer to God.

We cannot leave this study of biblical and theological directions for change without adding that more is involved here than the distribution of material goods. A *third* major criterion is the fullest possible freedom for every person on earth. Such liberty is more than economic opportunity, though that is part of it. Liberty also includes participation in the making of those decisions by which one's total welfare is affected. There can be a hoarding of power as well as of wealth. There are now too few who make decisions and issue orders, and too many who receive the orders and are expected simply to obey. Any thoroughly new society must add political freedom to economic opportunity.

The Hebrews were commanded not to oppress others, but to remember their own slavery in Egypt (Exodus 23:9). God's demand to the Egyptian Pharaoh—"Let my people go" (Exod. 5:1)—is to be addressed to tyrants everywhere. The inscription on our own Liberty Bell was taken from Leviticus 25:10 "Proclaim liberty throughout the land to all its inhabitants." Ecclesiastes (4:13) saw the dead as more fortunate than the living because "there was power" on the side of the oppressors while the oppressed "had no one to comfort them." Isaiah represented God as wanting worshipers "to undo the thongs of the yoke, to let the oppressed go free, and to break every yoke" (Isa. 58:6). Jesus, in his Nazareth statement, took up the long struggle "to proclaim release to the captives, to set at liberty those who are oppressed" (Luke 4:16-19).

God created persons as something more than puppets. God does not coercively jerk us about with attached strings. God establishes relationships with persons as free beings who can respond or rebel. Persons are so made as to grow through the responsible exercise of freedom. The full realization of human potentiality requires the maximum autonomy consistent with the freedom of others. Today the world has not only technological resources for the relief of poverty, but also social inventions for the sharing of freedom. Yet we have lacked the motive and the will to use both of these capabilities. We have remained too much a self-indulgent people, placing personal satisfaction ahead of religious and social innovation. As I wrote on another occasion, "Our culture too much embodies affluence without altruism and technology without transcendent reference. We are specialists without purpose and sensualists without heart."[7] This will no longer do in a day of nuclear weaponry, revolution in the Third World, and threatened collapse of environmental support.

QUESTIONS FOR DISCUSSION
1. Fantasize on the kind of world suggested by Isaiah 58:6-12. Compare your mental picture with recent newspaper or television reports which suggest characteristics of our present world. What are the greatest contrasts you see?

2. Do you agree with Emerson's statement about the possibilities in difficult revolutionary situations? What do you think should be the unique contributions of Christians to such times?

3. What is your reaction to the assertion that both the Bible and our basic theological beliefs require continuous personal and social change? In the section on "Change and the Christian Heritage," do the suggested six consequences go too far or not far enough?

4. List in one column what you consider to be important Christian guidelines for social and economic life (those discussed under "Criteria for Change" or your revision of that list). List in a second column the guidelines which you feel are actually followed by society at each of these points. Discuss agreements and disagreements.

5. Since, in comparison with other peoples, we are the wealthy of the earth, it has been suggested that America's number one *spiritual* problem is "How can a rich person enter the kingdom of God?" How would you answer this in the light of Matthew 19:16-24 (Jesus and the rich young ruler)? Do you agree that working for more economic resources for the poor also contributes to the spiritual salvation of the rich?

PROJECTS FOR ACTION
1. Begin keeping a regular meditation time as a counterforce to the pressures of culture. Each day read some of the Bible passages suggested in this chapter, meditate on their meaning for your own actions, and express your petitions and dedication in prayer.

2. Talk to your family or to other suitable groups about the insights gained from the above chapter, thus spreading the impact of your study.

3. Invite friends to the next session of this study/action group, thus involving more persons in this unit of Doing the Word.

4. If you have friends who occupationally help form public opinion—as educators, publicists, business persons, or political leaders—see where they stand on the Christian principles discussed above. Invite them to consider these guidelines more seriously.

5. Plan a display of information and pictures on the gap between rich and poor in the world and in your community. Suggestions for resource material can be obtained from local librarians, poverty action groups, social studies teachers, and national public affairs organizations. Also consult the session plans at the end of this book.

6. Outline the chief features of your present church program. Relying on memory or available newsletter files, compare these with your church's program five or ten years ago. Has the program changed to deal with new social needs, especially of the disprivileged? Or study the annual budget of your church. Approximately what percentage of expenditures would you estimate is used to serve (1) the more fortunate members of our society, and (2) the poor? Is this budget biblical? Report your findings to your group.

CHAPTER 2
INVITATIONS TO INNOVATION

Many people still living can remember traveling in horse-drawn buggies, reading by kerosene lamps, attending one-room schools, and patronizing general stores with potbellied stoves. Within a single lifetime we have come to spaceships landing on the moon, laser beams to outer space, internationalized multiversities, and computerized business. Over much of the world, modern technological culture is replacing an agricultural civilization that had been with us since almost the beginning of recorded history. As indicated by several statistical measures of human achievements, as much has happened during the last generation as in all previous history.[8] In some fields the accumulation of human knowledge is doubling every five or six years.

The social setting for human life has been so decisively altered as to force a rethinking of much we had thought securely settled. Unprecedented changes have already produced basic alterations in our economic system. Through powerful labor unions, workers have a greater voice in management decisions. In many areas, huge corporations have destroyed the preconditions for laissez faire competition. Government policies increasingly affect personal incomes, business decisions, and international events. Technological inventions have altered the nature of living and the prospects of the future environment.

A COMPASSIONATE VIEW OF STATISTICS
Rapid change has also piled up new problems. Not all of our past difficulties have been resolved. Continuing human tragedies require further transformation both of systemic structures and of individual attitudes and lifestyles.

Serious economic inequality continues to keep some in poverty and others in wealth. Virtually unchanged for the last twenty-five years in the United States is a maldistribution of income that allows 3 percent of consumer units (families and independent individuals) to receive 18 percent of the total income, while 23 percent must be content with 4 percent. (Recession in the seventies has made the problem worse.) Inequalities in ownership of wealth are even greater. It is estimated that the richest one half of 1 percent of United States consumer units own about 22 percent of the country's wealth, while the poorest 26 percent own less than one half of 1 percent.[9] For a graphic representation of the distribution of wealth, we might consider the United States banquet table so arranged that each chair represents 5 percent of the population and each plate 5 percent of the wealth. The pattern, enforced by the police, would be one person eating from something over ten plates, the next two from approximately four plates, the next eight from five, and the other nine sharing half a plate. If any family tried that way of serving meals, we can imagine the consequences for harmony, order, and decorous behavior.

Whenever one reads such statistics with an informed mind as well as a loving heart, additional meanings are added. Poverty also means inadequate diet, poor housing, less education, undeveloped potential, and family strains, along with continuous fear of medical bills, rent increases, and unemployment. It means babies exposed to rats, and adolescents influenced by gangs. It means helplessness and humiliation, enduring the knowledge that others live in advantaged neighborhoods and are able to give opportunities to their children. For "wealth" read also luxuries and political power, along with the temptation to materialism, pride, and moral blindness.

We sometimes think that by progressive income taxes we are reducing inequality. But other taxes, like sales and property and social security taxes that are levied at the same rate for rich and poor alike, actually hit the poor harder because they spend a greater proportion of their incomes on these items. In addition, loopholes allow persons with higher incomes to escape much of the steeper taxation. A calculation of the combined results in 1965 showed that the one third of United States families with the lowest income paid 30 percent in federal, state, and local taxes. The one third middle-incomes paid 26 percent and the top one third 33 percent.

DISTRIBUTION OF FAMILIES AND TAXES BY INCOME GROUP, 1965 (Derived from unpublished data provided by the Council of Economic Advisors)

In 1965 the median income was $7,000 per year and the middle income group ($5,000 to $9,000 per year) paid a smaller percentage of its income as tax than the other groups.

Income Group	Percent of Families	Percent of Taxes Paid	Taxes as a Percent of Income
Below middle	33	16	30
Middle	33	24	26
Above middle	33	60	33
Total	100	100	31 (av)

Income excludes transfer payments, but includes capital gains and corporate profits. Taxes consist of all federal, state, and local taxes.

Those at the very bottom of the lowest third, with incomes under $2,000, paid 44 percent of their income in taxes. This is a reversal of Robin Hood, by taking from the poor and favoring the rich.[10] Welfare payments to the poor may relieve the picture somewhat, but there is also "welfare" for the rich in subsidies and allowances to the oil industry, defense firms, large farmers, railroads and airlines. Or we often provide better schools, streets, and fire and police protection in more prosperous areas.[11]

Equality of opportunity is even less evident on a world scale. While the gross national product for the United States in 1972 amounted to $5,590 per capita, for India the figure was $110 and for Indonesia $90. Life expectancy for the industrially developed nations is about 71 years, and for less developed countries 53 years. (See Chart 1, p. 26.)

Robert L. Heilbroner dramatically outlined the changes that would take place if an American suburban family were magically changed into a typical family in the developing world. Their house would first be stripped of its furniture, except for a few frayed blankets, one chair, and a simple kitchen table. All clothes would go, except for the oldest outfit each owned. Only the head of the family could keep a pair of shoes. With all utilities and kitchen appliances would go the contents of the cupboards, except for a small bag of flour, some moldy potatoes, and a few onions. Then the house itself would be taken away and the family moved into the toolshed. There would no longer be mail delivery or a fire department. A two-classroom school would be three miles away, and a midwife-staffed hospital ten miles distant. The family might keep five dollars, but with replenishment of that amount always in doubt.[12]

The gap between rich and poor in the world is getting worse. From 1960 to 1970 the average per capita income increased 27 percent in the poor countries, but 43 percent in the developed countries. When income figures are so much lower to start with, it takes a much higher percentage of increase for poor countries before they begin to catch

Chart 1
THE DEVELOPMENT GAP

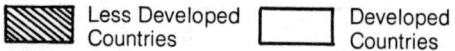

THE LESS DEVELOPED COUNTRIES HAVE...

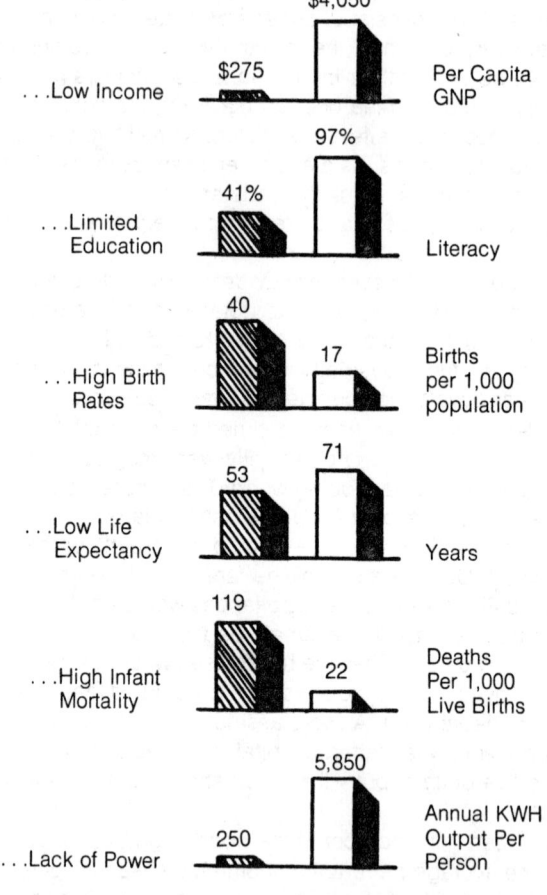

The differences between developed and developing countries are shown here.

1974 estimates, from *War on Hunger,* December 1974. Source: U.S. Agency for International Development.

up. Unless there are heroic rescue operations, those countries in the worst condition (the "Fourth World") actually face negative growth in the next few years, rather than any increase at all.[13]

WASTING SCARCE RESOURCES
Alongside poverty and inequality we still suffer from alarming waste. Too many brands or models of essentially the same product unnecessarily duplicate facilities or transportation. Manufacturing useless or harmful goods reduces resources available for needs of the poor. Idle production facilities and unemployed persons during recessions reduce output. Planned obsolescence, or "death-dating," cuts quality to force early replacement. This may create a junkman's paradise, but also an earth depleted of natural resources. A population that blindly follows style changes, throws out clothes by the closetful and cars by the garageful. While there are some legitimate uses for advertising, it becomes wasteful when it encourages unnecessary expenditures, popularizes materialism, or encourages mass hedonism. It is not a sound argument to define advertising as necessary to protect mass production and jobs, when masses of the poor need different products the manufacture of which would also protect production and jobs.

Military expenditures constitute one of the world's worst economic wastes. This is true even though one might successfully argue that we do need responsible military protection in the present insecure world. Even so, unnecessary overkill capacity, redundant weapons systems, and excess defense facilities cannot be justified. Insofar as the nations of the world delay in discovering or accepting other means toward peace and security, they are diverting massive amounts of resources from urgent human needs. With respect to the Mekong Delta project, with its potential for feeding the hungry in Southeast Asia, Lester B. Pearson said, "It would make the angels weep to think that less than one third of the money that has been spent in one year by the United States in the prosecution of the Vietnam war would complete this wonderfully imaginative project."[14]

Massive drain on irreplaceable raw materials cannot long continue without dangerous resource depletion. Persistent population increase will multiply the number of mouths to feed, the quantity of steel going into apartment buildings, and the number of cars polluting the atmosphere. The drive of a traditional economy toward expansion will also subtract from resources and add to the filth we dump into the sky and waterways. Modern persons are born into the "concrete cradle" of the city, which may also become their technological tomb. Human beings are becoming an endangered species in a world created by God for the benefit of human beings.

THREATS TO FREEDOM
New economic arrangements are also necessary to reduce increasing threats to freedom. Traditional capitalist theory held that the consumer was king—manufacturers and distributors bowed down to consumers because consumers decided what to buy. This theory is now in question. Obviously producers do take sales into account in their policy decisions. But the freedom of consumers is decidedly limited. They may be advisers at court, but they are not kings.

Consumers can choose only from among the products offered for sale. They have no effective way to say, for example, that they would prefer fewer brands and models for the sake of the savings that would be possible if only one or a few standard models were manufactured. Furthermore, a huge volume of advertising hides or distorts information that consumers need to register their true preferences. An election is not very democratic if only one party can issue its publicity. In addition, not all consumers have an equal "vote" in allocating their purchasing power. The wants of the rich are backed by more dollars in the marketplace than are the needs of the poor. Production of diamonds and large cars is likely to be overvalued while cheap mass transportation is undervalued. Economic freedom still requires a better system of participatory democracy for consumers—which is to say, for all citizens, since we are all consumers.

Concentration of power in large economic organizations also threatens liberty. Unless there are effective checks by the total citizenry, labor unions and professional associations can become centers of entrenched power. In large corporations, shareholders' democracy does not effectively exist. Stock ownership is too widely scattered for effective debate of issues before decisions are made. It is now standard economic theory to recognize a separation of ownership from control in huge corporations. A comparatively few persons control vast empires. This now becomes an even greater factor with the appearance of conglomerates (engaged in diversified enterprises) and multinational corporations (doing business in many countries). The annual production of General Motors has been calculated to exceed the gross national product of Belgium or Switzerland, while Standard Oil of New Jersey (Exxon) sales are larger than the gross national product of Denmark or Austria.[15] We may well have nightmares about the possibilities of a comparatively small group of persons shaping the economy of the world and powerfully influencing international political decisions.

The economically powerful are also likely to have disproportionate influence in the courts, schools, legislatures, and government offices. Because of such influence, United Funds have recently been criticized for favoring agencies serving middle-class Whites, and neglecting innovative agencies working, for example, to eliminate poverty. Recent revelations concerning Watergate, Chile, the CIA, and the military-industrial complex underscore widespread modern threats to freedom. We very much need economic relationships on a world scale that will sustain and strengthen democracy, rather than weaken and undermine it.

Our persistent major problems of poverty and inequality, waste, environmental pollution and depletion, and threats to freedom become even more serious when judged from biblical and theological perspectives. *Compare the content of the first part of this chapter with the latter part of the preceding chapter.* The Christian motivation of love requires equal opportunity for all, the careful use of God's resources for human need, and the fullest possible freedom for each person. When the calling of God is heard amid the accumulation of modern misery, we have a powerful moral imperative to support change.

DEEPLY ROOTED DEFECTS

Patching up old structures with superficial improvements is not enough. Some basic defects of socioeconomic systems are among the causes of our present difficulties. For this reason, increasing numbers of persons are talking about a new economic order. For example, our classical method for dealing with poverty has been charity, as in private philanthropy, United Funds, or church funds for disaster relief. Short-term relief is imperative, but it is not enough. Such charity can become paternalistic, in that it denies certain freedoms to the recipients. The donors unilaterally decide how much is to be given and to which causes. Typically such philanthropy treats only the symptoms or results of a deeper disease. Now we see that all have a right to be involved in adopting policies that will not only relieve immediate suffering, but by getting at causes, will also remove future distress.

A more basic cause of our economic troubles is our exaggerated historic myth that an unregulated free enterprise system will cure all ills. This laissez faire (or "let alone") type of capitalism assumed that the free action of many individuals, each seeking to maximize personal gratifications, would automatically add up to the greatest common good. This transmutation was to be made through market prices fluctuating in response to supply and demand—and thereby attracting natural resources, capital, and labor where they were most needed, and also stimulating efficiency and improvement as each tried to get ahead of competitors. This system, though never completely unregulated, did indeed allow spectacular economic progress in the past. It provided considerable freedom and allowed complex decisions to be made with minimal external controls. As will be further elaborated in Chapter 4, there is still an important place for the mechanisms of a free market. But it is becoming clear to economists and populations alike that such a system alone cannot now deliver us from the kind of tragedies described earlier in this chapter.

For one thing, the successful operation of this system depended upon perpetuating a situation of many independent buyers and sellers, no one of which had a large enough influence unilaterally to control price. However, the operation of the system itself naturally resulted in those successful in competition growing larger. The trend toward big corporations was also speeded up by the requirements of modern technology for specialized personnel, vast capital accumulation, and costly research. In many parts of the economy we cannot get the efficiency that we now want without violating the conditions necessary for the old system. For this reason, as John Kenneth Galbraith once put it, "The foreign visitor, brought to the United States to study American production methods and associated marvels, visits the same firms as do attorneys of the Department of Justice in their search for monopoly."[16] Even though there are limits to the efficiency of size, varying with the type of enterprise, we will continue to have business units of such size and power that an increasingly regulated system will be necessary.

A market economy tends to increase the inequalities, once the trend toward concentration has started. In the large section of the economy in which this applies, those who have become stronger have advantages in future competition, which make them still bigger. According to Richard Lichtman, "It is as though after every race the runners were permitted to start again from the positions in which they found themselves at the termination of the previous race."[17]

Advocates of the old system made a fundamental mistake when they assumed that the greatest possible liberty could be secured by letting each person do what seemed right, without external restraint. This can be illustrated in the frontier community before the establishment of "law and order." Originally everyone could do what he or she wished, but it was not long before the most fortunate or the most unscrupulous or the most efficient (in multiplying cattle or in handling a gun—or in both) became dominant. Most citizens then could exercise freedom only with the permission of the strongest. Essentially the same thing has happened in economic affairs. For the frontier community, a solution was found in the introduction of a democratic system of laws. We are still groping for an economic solution.

Another change which has made our classical system impossible is the very government regulation we have adopted to make the economy tolerable. We are not likely to change our minds about the necessity of such governmental guidance for the economy. While we may argue about this or that detail, genuine imperfections in the system have had to be dealt with. Not only workers and consumers, but also business executives in general have wanted some kinds of help. In some cases government has assumed more of the risks of business, while private industry still takes the profits. Examples include: guaranteeing bank loans to some corporations facing bankruptcy, covering unexpected costs for defense contractors, providing subsidies to shipping firms to allow them to meet foreign competition, and forming Amtrak and Conrail to take over losses on railroad passenger service. Of particular interest to the other groups in society are government actions like minimum wage laws, social security systems, provision of schools, or consumer protection legislation. This is not unregulated free enterprise. We have already moved far beyond classical capitalism to a mixed economy. But the present "mix" still leaves us with serious problems, and we continue to search for new directions.

Besides the change in conditions that made the old system impossible, it always had certain inherent defects with which we have not yet fully dealt—and which have profound religious and ethical dimensions. One of these is that the processes of the market cannot measure the full range of value. There are qualitative benefits that cannot be calculated in a quantitative price. Using the ability to make a profit as the test for continued production limits our ability to reach other humane goals. Some things, like bridges, roads, libraries, and parks, may be very valuable though not easily profitable. The quality of television programs, the dangers of pollution, or relational values like love and justice, do not register adequately in the price system and therefore in economic decisions.

Furthermore, the automatic operation of the free market depended upon all persons seeking maximum returns for themselves in competition with others. This expectation still looms large in our current system. Dependence on competitiveness produces some gains, but it also has grievous shortcomings. Competition is a win-lose mechanism that may not be related to competence or service. Chance or accident plays a part (including fortunate inheritances from relatives), and the unsuccessful may suffer through no fault of their own. Those bankrupted are not necessarily unfit for superior production. They may simply be unfit for stooping to the deceit or manipulation necessary for success in some situations. As well as sometimes stimulating improvement, competition can also pull all competitors to the level of the lowest. When consumers have neither testing apparatus nor complete records, misleading advertising or shoddy merchandising may be so profitable that it has to be imitated for even a better-intentioned person to stay in business.

Rather than being held suspect, the pursuit of private wealth is now encouraged. Success in acquisition is honored by favorable publicity and higher status. Yet egoism is inherently exploitative, because the interests of others are subordinated to one's own gain. Choosing the easiest job at the highest pay, instead of working up to one's highest capacity at the place of greatest social need, is robbing society. Most of us would stay away from a doctor whose chief source of satisfaction was making more money. We would refuse to vote for a presidential candidate who was simply competing for a higher-paying job. Why do we then support an economic tradition that depends upon egoistic drives?

Furthermore, there has always been an inherent instability in a profit-motivated, competitive system, as illustrated in business cycles of prosperity and depression. One dynamic involved in these booms and busts is this: As each producer plans for greater production and profits, all producers together periodically exceed the amount that would be profitably bought at current demand. This can be illustrated in the fanciful parable of the nine ships and the one cargo. In a time of prosperity no shipowner had an empty ship. A single cargo went to each of nine shipowners asking in vain to be carried. After the cargo departed, each shipowner (being acquisitively motivated, and under competitive conditions having no accurate knowledge of competitors' plans) concluded that he could make additional profit by building another ship. The result was that nine ships were built, but there was only one cargo to be carried. To pay the bills, workers had to be laid off, which meant less purchasing power and still fewer cargoes to be shipped. This forced still more laying off of workers in an all too familiar downward spiral.

Collective greed and self-centered competition also drive toward a quicker exhaustion of natural resources. A useful illustration is that of the commons, or open grazing ground. All villagers are allowed to use the commons, and all act acquisitively and competitively. Therefore it is always to the best interests of each (1) that the total number of cattle grazing not be so great as to exhaust the grass, and (2) that the number of his or her own cattle be as great as possible. As each seeks the second end, all together periodically violate the first. Under frontier conditions, when the population was small and the wilderness seemingly inexhaustible, each farmer could compete against others in clearing the most possible private acreage, and the interests of society for additional farmland could simultaneously be served. But under present conditions of limited resources, we can no longer afford the old approach to the commons. The monitors of planetary resources join the witness of biblical prophets in condemning acquisitive competition and in supporting a new way of cooperation, compassion, and the simple life.

The competitiveness and acquisitiveness that cause trouble economically are also qualities that raise questions ethically. In the words of Richard K. Taylor, "Jesus turns values topsy-turvy, teaching that the leader must be a servant, the great must be humble, the rich must be those of few possessions."[18] By turning commonly accepted values upside down, Jesus sets our value structure right side up.

Enlightenment on these matters is growing. Yet, as *Newsweek* put it, "While corporate America has come to recognize certain social responsibilities, it still feels far more comfortable with Adam Smith than it does with Ralph Nader."[19] The same thing can perhaps still be said about the general public. Our own affluence still blinds us to the sufferings of others, and also to the economic and spiritual deprivations that we ourselves suffer. Rubem Alves, a Latin American theologian, suggests that if we were shut up in a room with no windows or doors, we would try to find a way of escape. But we live in a castle with a thousand and one luxurious rooms, each filled with pleasures and surprises. When we get tired of one room, we move to another. Being so absorbed, no one notices that there is no way out of the castle. We are equally prisoners, although we can grow old without realizing it.[20]

Before the entire castle blows up, we had better take two quotations seriously. To those who have "great and goodly cities" and "houses full of all good things" Deuteronomy (6:10-12) proclaims, "When you eat and are full, then take heed lest you forget the Lord." A second reflection on our condition is from George B. Leonard: "Not to dream more boldly may turn out to be, in view of present realities, simply irresponsible."

QUESTIONS FOR DISCUSSION

1. List *and evaluate* all the arguments you can think of for and against the present inequality of income and wealth. For example, to the humanitarian arguments against poverty, it might be replied that raising standards of living would greatly increase pollution. The rejoinder to the claim of every person to God's creation might be that those who do not work should not eat. It can be argued that expenditures of the

rich provide jobs. Replies might be that crime also creates jobs for prison guards, or that producing what is needed by the poor would also provide jobs. To the argument that wealth is necessary for capital accumulation, it can be said that capital can come from other sources, such as corporate earnings, or loans, or greater investment by those whose incomes would be raised.

2. Are the present high salaries justified for movie stars and sports heroes? Give reasons for your answer.

3. Do you agree that illustrations of waste in this chapter are actually wasteful? What illustrations would you add?

4. The preceding chapters indicated both gains and losses under our traditional economic system. List in two columns the gains and losses as you see them. Is it possible to keep the desirable features and at the same time to improve the imperfections?

5. Certain outcomes were suggested above as inevitable in any acquisitively-motivated, competitive system. Do you agree? To break this dismal cycle, what Christian ethical principles need to be applied (or approximated) in economic life?

PROJECTS FOR ACTION

1. Drive through the poorest section in your city. List all the reasons you would not want to live there with your family—and add other reasons that are not apparent in casual observation. You might do the same for the wealthiest section. Are they both undesirable neighborhoods?

2. Try living for a week on the food budget of a family whose income is below the poverty level. Remember that even then you have not fully experienced the life of the poor. You have continued to live in your same house and neighborhood, to hold the same job, and to know that at the end of the week you would return to your old diet.

3. To replicate world conditions, serve a church supper with tables representing the United States and Europe receiving a sumptuous meal, and with large garbage cans evident. At most tables, representing Asia, Africa, and Latin America, serve an excellent meal to one person, and only bowls of soup to the others. Distribute a sheet summarizing economic differences between the developed and the developing worlds.[21]

4. Localize the problem by finding out (from welfare department, social security office, or census reports) how many unemployed there are in your community, and what is the distribution of local income, housing, and social facilities. Ask your informants how you can help.

5. What valid measures for aid to the poor or unemployed are cur-

rently before your state or national legislature? Write legislators indicating support.

6. What consumer protection agencies are available in your community (specialized newspaper or television reporters, government agencies, better business bureaus)? Support and publicize the best of these.

CHAPTER 3
UNACCEPTABLE MODELS FOR CHANGE

On the evening of November 6, 1917, revolutionary forces were attacking the former winter palace of the Czars. At 2:10 the next morning, invaders broke into an inner room of the palace where, around a single lamp burning on a table with its light shut off from the windows by newspapers, were seated the ministers of the provisional government. As the crowd burst into the room, their leader, a slight figure in a broad-brimmed hat, announced, "In the name of the Military Revolutionary Committee I declare you arrested." The Russian Revolution had reached its climax. The triumph of the Bolsheviki had begun.

A Chinese farmer in Hunan province, named Mao Tse-tung, became a Marxist and began organizing the peasants in Kiangsi. After the Long March to northern Shensi, and after the Japanese defeat in World War II, Communist armies in China shifted from guerilla tactics to civil war, and finally defeated the "Nationalist" armies under Chiang Kai-shek. In September, 1949, in Peiping's imperial palace, under the golden tiles of bygone dynasties, Mao Tse-tung proclaimed the establishment of the People's Republic of China.

On October 28, 1922, Rome, the city which was once the capital of the Caesars, witnessed invasion by a new kind of legions. Blackshirted Fascists poured into the city, armed with weapons ranging from clubs to machine guns. In other important cities of Italy the city halls, railway stations, and post offices had already been occupied. King Victor Emmanuel, fearing that the army would not resist the Blackshirts, telephoned the leader of the rebels, a newspaper editor waiting in his office in Milan, and asked him to become prime minister of Italy. Benito Mussolini thereupon crossed the Rubicon in a sleeping car, formed his cabinet in seven hours, and a short time later *Il Duce* became dictator of Italy.

At a few minutes before nine o'clock on Monday evening, February 27, 1933, a philosophy student at the University of Berlin was walking home through the snow. Passing the Reichstag building, meeting place of the German legislature, he heard the sound of breaking glass and saw a man with a torch on a first floor balcony. Police moved in to find the entire interior ablaze. Hermann Göring, Prussian Minister of the Interior, rushed from his office on Unter den Linden and declared at once that the conflagration was the result of a communist plot. Adolf Hitler, driving up with Goebbels, announced that this was "a sign from heaven," sent to show the German people what destruction would follow if the Communists came to power. No Communist connection with the burning of the Reichstag was ever established, and world opinion has long since believed that the Nazis themselves set it ablaze; but before morning four or five thousand leading Communists and Socialists were arrested. In an atmosphere of intimidation and terrorism Germans went to the polls to give the Nazis sufficient support for those swift measures which made Hitler dictator of Germany.

Somewhat similar scenarios have been played out in country after country around the world. One might speak of Czechoslovakia, Chile, India, Peru, Panama, South Africa, Rhodesia, Indonesia, Nigeria, Vietnam, Cambodia, Korea, Portugal, Angola. One might speak of assassinations, guerillas, military coups, power struggles. Leftist or rightist dictatorships, veering more or less toward communism on the one hand or fascism on the other, continue to threaten liberal democracy. Communist movements we continue to expect. But we tend to assign fascism to past decades and to disregard similar manifestations under other names in various contemporary movements. These two general options are taken very seriously by a large part of the world's population. While there is considerable variation among national expressions of these two tendencies, there are also general similarities that allow evaluation of their possibilities or perils.

COMMUNIST AND FASCIST-TYPE OPTIONS

Unlike other modern social systems, which tend to be neutral on philosophical or religious matters, classical communism was based on a definite metaphysical position—that of dialectical materialism. This philosophy has often supported antireligious emphases in communist countries. Churches might be left free to worship, but not to seek converts. There have been some recent accommodations, and the situation is freer in some countries than others. Nevertheless, there are still strict limits to the freedom of churches in public affairs. Fascistic regimes have often claimed to be friendly to religion, but they also have forbidden the kind of basic social criticism that is a central function of the church. In somewhat different ways, both types of dictatorship have undermined a free church.

With respect to political theory, the Communist Manifesto proclaimed, "The history of all hitherto existing society is the history of class struggles." A Marxist insists that the political state is the instrument of oppression used by the economically dominant class. In a capitalist society, what is called a democracy is in effect a capitalist dictatorship. There it is believed that the proletariat must seize and reshape existing state machinery. The dictatorship of the bourgeoisie must be replaced by the dictatorship of the proletariat. This is considered an expansion of liberty, since it substitutes for the minority rule of the capitalists, the majority rule of the workers. Therefore, Communists make the claim that so exasperates the Western world, namely that there is more political freedom under communism than there is under capitalism

Theoretically there is to be greater future liberty in the communist society, including the utopian notion of a future "withering away" of the state. In several communist countries there has been some relaxation of centralized controls. Policies of terror have been moderated, and a somewhat wider range of criticism is allowed. But even sixty years of Soviet history have produced all too little progress in this regard, as Alexander Dubcek in Czechoslovakia discovered when he tried to create "socialism with a human face," or as Soviet recipients of the Nobel Peace prize have learned. For them the price of dissidence was exile.

Fascist-type dictatorships have also substituted the totalitarian state for the sovereign people. The contrast is summarized in two statements. Abraham Lincoln spoke of "government of the people, by the people, for the people." Mussolini's comparable statement was "everything in the state, nothing against the state, nothing outside the state." The latter process was described in the German "Fuhrerprinzip," which insisted that authority flow from the top down and obedience from the bottom up—again the direct opposite from democratic aspirations.

Both communism and fascism have seen violence as normally necessary to gain power. This is followed by ruthless suppression of opposition. As Mao Tse-tung put it, "A revolution is not a dinner party." Not only does the state dominate the individual, but also all organizations within it.

In economic affairs, the typical communist pattern has been state ownership of substantially all of the means of production, and coordinated management under a comprehensive system of planning. Production goals are fixed, and resources are allocated in the light of priorities established by the group holding dictatorial power. Extreme and inefficient as their system has often been, Communists have frequently exhibited a notable passion for economic justice. They promise opportunity for the poor, medical and social welfare measures, and the extension of education. The communist promise carries conviction to millions of the dispossessed, especially when hearers are under the domination of landlords and are neglected by reactionary, dictatorial governments. To pretend that this is not so is to blind ourselves to an important fact of modern life.

The economic system of fascist-type societies can best be described as maintaining essential features and privileges of the traditional economy, but under totalitarian state control. Extreme rightists have bitterly opposed both socialism and communism. They have retained economic enterprises predominantly under private ownership. Maximization of profit has remained a major motive. Competition, though less free, was still an important regulator. While these fundamentals of capitalism were retained under fascism, strict state control was introduced at points thought necessary for stability and progress. Some concessions might be made to the masses at the same time that the chief prerogatives of the privileged were maintained.

Communism is the marriage between totalitarianism and a revolutionary program aimed at power for the disprivileged through widespread socialization. Fascism uses political dictatorship to freeze the status quo as much as possible—or to move back toward an older system with less socialization.

The usual charting of social systems is on a one-dimensional straight line ranging from reactionary dictatorships to communism. Fitted in between are varying degrees of conservatism and liberalism. This pattern neglects the likenesses at the extremes. While they differ in economic approach, communism and fascism both share a totalitarian political structure. To represent contemporary alternatives more accurately would require a two-dimensional table. (See Chart 2.) The columns would represent our basic economic choice between a more completely laissez-faire individualism, and greater government initiative and regulation. The rows would represent our basic political choice between democracy and dictatorship. Drawn on this four cell chart, the spectrum of our public options becomes not a straight line, but something more like a horseshoe.

One can understand the temporary need for more authoritarian governments in countries that lack the necessary educational or communicational base to sustain democracy. Especially when dictatorships are already in power, a measure of violence may also be necessary for revolution in some countries. We would have to admit that

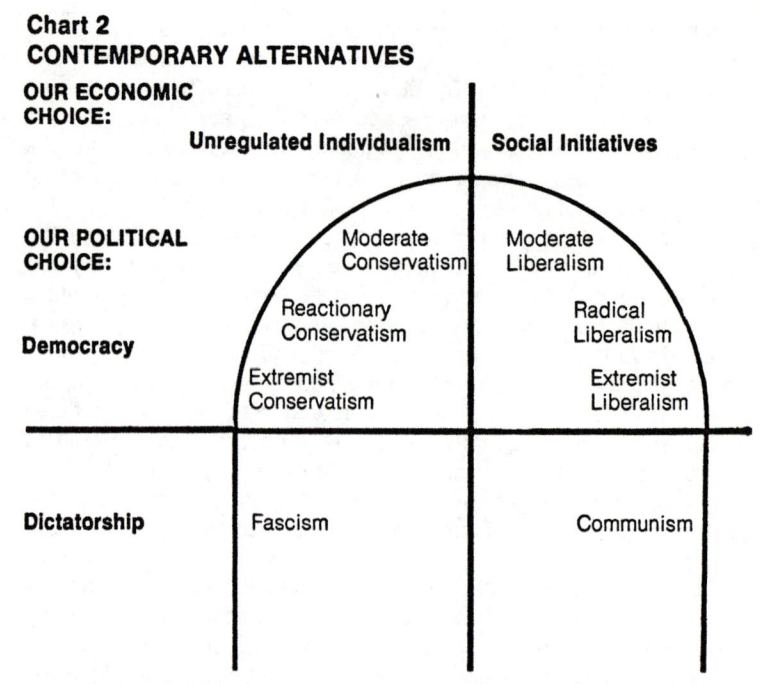

Chart 2
CONTEMPORARY ALTERNATIVES

OUR ECONOMIC CHOICE:

	Unregulated Individualism	Social Initiatives
OUR POLITICAL CHOICE: **Democracy**	Moderate Conservatism Reactionary Conservatism Extremist Conservatism	Moderate Liberalism Radical Liberalism Extremist Liberalism
Dictatorship	Fascism	Communism

some forms of violence are already involved in our present system. Yet the technology of violence is now so ominous, the tenacity of totalitarianism so great, and the extreme economic measures of both communism and fascism so limited in their possibilities, that well-established democracies should be able to find a better way to even more thoroughgoing improvements.

GROWING TOTALITARIAN THREATS

Because the dangers of extremist dictatorship are so great, it becomes important to raise the question of indicators or warning signals. What are the deceptive poses of politicians and propagandists that we need to watch out for if we cherish our liberties? Although we have strong historical bulwarks against totalitarian threats, we need to remember how quickly and unexpectedly such movements triumphed in other countries. Only a few months separated Lenin the exile in the home of a Zurich shoemaker and Lenin the head of the first Council of People's Commissars in Russia. Mussolini founded his newspaper *Popolo d'Italia* in a garret room only eight years before he became dictator of Italy. When the Nazi vote in Germany fell drastically in the

November, 1932, elections, this was hailed as "the final annihilation of Hitler." Three months later he became chancellor.

In all these cases major crises deepened popular disillusionment, desperation, and readiness to accept drastic remedies as a last resort. What would happen in our own country if we experienced a deeper economic depression, the beginning of environmental collapse, runaway inflation, or a long, decimating war, perhaps resulting in defeat? Would we then have sufficient democratic resources to meet one or a combination of such public crises?

The best way, of course, to avoid disaster is to solve problems as they appear. The only way to prevent the piling up of discontent which will demand more extremist solutions, is to eliminate the causes of the discontent. This would be equivalent to turning off the gas, rather than trying to clamp the lid on the boiling pot—which simply insures an explosion. Democratic society must find ways to meet basic human needs like poverty, loneliness, discrimination, anxiety, alienation, and frustration. Not to do so is to prepare the way for totalitarianism. Those opposing the necessary changes become the laborers laying the tracks over which the trains of the dictators will later run.

Especially in these times of rapid social change, adequate programs need to move farther faster than ever before. In terms of the options on Chart 2, it takes only a few years for what was once a conservative position to become reactionary. What was once liberal soon becomes conservative. Avoiding totalitarianism depends on how rapidly we are willing to progress toward human welfare within democratic processes. In a very real sense it is the old regime which determines whether violence will occur, by whether or not it is willing to accept necessary reform. As John F. Kennedy put it, "Those who make peaceful revolution impossible will make violent revolution inevitable."

The possibility of totalitarianism is also increased, perhaps unintentionally, by methods which undermine the foundations of freedom. Democracy by definition requires at least three things: civil liberties (such as freedom of speech and the press), equal suffrage ("one person, one vote"), and decision by majorities. Each of these has recently been under attack, sometimes by highly placed officials. The entire Watergate syndrome was ominous in this regard. Yet similar atrocities had happened before, and have been revealed since. Some recent revelations of domestic spying by the CIA and the FBI show how our democratic traditions can be undermined.

Some leaders have tried to eliminate free discussion by contriving a monopoly of expression for themselves. The method has been not assassination or imprisonment, but intimidation and manipulation. In 1950 Joseph McCarthy introduced the "nightmare decade" with the words, "I have here in my hand a list . . . "[22] The subsequent silencing of opponents and termination of careers will long live in infamy. Others also followed the formula of falsely and slanderously identifying their opponents with whatever was unpopular at the moment, whether that was communism, crime and violence, or radicalism in general. Or by skillful public relations techniques candidates might falsely identify themselves with what was popular at the moment, such as liberalism or reform—even as the German Nazi party inaccurately used the word "socialist" in its title, and as some communist governments identify themselves as "democratic republics." Similarly our own country has had "peace" candidates who actually went to war, or "law and order" proposals that violated the spirit of the Constitution. By such deliberately confusing tactics, governments are elected and policies determined, not by the will of the people, but by the skill of advertising agencies and the capacity of candidates for immorality.

Other ways of silencing the opposition or nullifying the will of the majority include shouting down speakers or breaking up meetings, "dirty tricks," lists of "enemies" marked for harassment by government agencies, and schemes to withhold vital information from the public. Threats of loss of jobs or television licenses can have a "chilling effect" on supporters of the opposition. By using official regulatory or law enforcement agencies during the Watergate period, and by allowing domestic spying, we began the politicalization of the police, which is a dream of every would-be dictator. From every housetop and television transmitter we must continuously shout that the democratic way for dealing with opposition is responsibly to speak against it. The totalitarian way is to silence it.

The rights of "one person, one vote," and of majorities to make decisions are denied also by any seriously disproportionate influence by a few. When large campaign contributors can manipulate behind the scenes and thus more easily gain the ear of officials, they are in effect stuffing the ballot box with extra votes. Furthermore, excessive centralization of power in the presidency limits decision-making by a Congress elected by the people.

The catalog of horrors is not yet complete. Extremists to right and to left have been busy undermining social institutions that are basically essential for a functioning democracy, such as schools, libraries, or churches. Democratically meeting emerging crises requires a high level of education, which is impossible without adequate educational agencies. It also requires public capacities to evaluate rapid change in the light of reliable norms, which is impossible without vital, prophetic churches. Yet persons even highly placed in public office have found it to their interests to weaken educational and religious institutions by rendering false charges, reducing available support, or by planting enough unfounded doubts in the minds of the citizenry to arouse a vague distrust of these basic institutions.

Responsible citizens must now demonstrate that any time a politician tries such tactics, he or she will be brought down in a landslide defeat. In addition, an intelligent electorate will support only those candidates who offer adequate and innovative programs for dealing rapidly enough with basic problems to prevent a buildup to a crisis that invites dictatorship.

DOMINATION BY ECONOMIC CONSOLIDATION

Another unacceptable model for the future is domination by huge concentrations of private economic power. This could become a different form of dictatorship, transferring centralized control from the seats of government to the board rooms of business. Instead of governments controlling concentrations of private economic power, governments would be controlled by a comparatively small economic elite, not only on economic matters but on many political matters. In such a situation freedom would be lost, while inequality and exploitation could be increased to serve the interests of the dominant few.

On a world scale this possibility is illustrated by the growth of huge multinational corporations. They have been very aggressively changing our economic order. If present trends continue, by the end of the next decade a few hundred corporations will control 50 to 80 percent of the essential factors of production in the non-communist world. Business units of the size here involved tend to have the powers of a monopoly. (Economists point out that "oligopoly," or a situation with only a few giants in a field, results also in essentially monopoly conditions.) Such "cosmocorps" can use profits from one country to drive out smaller competitors in other countries. Or they can use profits from one product, such as oil, to extend their power into coal or natural gas. Free enterprise would remain a partial reality only for those types of small business that still had an economic advantage. Apart from that, the system might be described as state welfare for big business. We have learned in recent experience how economic power can shape government policy to increase profits—and also how corporations that get "too big to fail" have a convincing claim to government aid to cover their losses. The same thing can happen on the world scene.

The problem posed by multinational corporations is not international economic enterprise as such. Multinationals have made many positive contributions in supplying capital, employment opportunities, and consumer goods. In numerous fields, large scale enterprise can reap savings through mass production, planned distribution, more research, and coordinated decisions. Both consumers and workers could share in these savings. As Richard Barnet and Ronald Müller point out, in *Global Reach: The Power of the Multinational Corporations,* "The men who run the global corporations are the first in history with the organization, technology, money, and ideology to make a credible try at managing the world as an integrated unit."[23] In a day of global interdependence requiring international cooperation, the global corporations propose to take charge.

The problem is not international enterprise, nor technical expertise. The problem is centralized control by comparatively small groups for private profit. This approach gives little attention to the common good. Global corporations can administer prices to the point of greatest profitability to themselves. This in a real sense is the ability to levy a tax on the consumers of the world.

As Adam Smith observed in *Wealth of Nations,* the holders of concentrated economic power who try "to widen the market and narrow the competition" can earn profits in excess of "what they would naturally be," and thus "levy for their own benefit an absurd tax upon the rest of their fellow citizens." A comparatively few decision-makers can generate international economic crises. They can shift production from high wage areas in the United States to low wage areas with 15 cents an hour jobs, such as in Taiwan or Haiti, and create "ghost towns" and "ghost nations." By advertising and by the selection of goods to be produced, they can control cultural development, standardizing for the entire world what people will eat, drink, and wear. Such cultural domination contradicts our growing appreciation of cultural pluralism. Furthermore, the drive to maximize profits could easily accelerate ecological destruction and the exhaustion of natural resources. Especially is this true now when the biggest profits are to be had from spreading to the world the unnecessary luxury and the overdeveloped materialistic lifestyle of the richest nations. Living standards do need to be raised in other parts of the world, but this does not include the overconsumption that finally becomes a blight rather than a blessing. The danger is that we export the worst features of an industrial culture along with the best. In such matters consumers pay the costs of their own exploitation.

Even if the motivation of private profit could miraculously be replaced by a universal dominance of altruistic attitudes, huge multinational corporations would still involve a denial of liberty. A small group, often outside one's own country, would be making life-changing decisions for the multitude. Given human nature as it is, we cannot give up the democratic goal of full participation in decision-making by all those whose welfare is affected. This is necessary not only to check the propensities toward selfishness in even the best of us, but to permit full autonomous growth, which is the right of every person.

The multinational corporation, one of the most powerful forces in shaping our future lives, is also one of the most difficult to control democratically. It can often unseat unfriendly governments, or evade the restrictions of one country by using the resources of another country. There are ways, for example, of shifting some tax obligations from one country to another with a more favorable rate. The United Nations provides no effective enforcement machinery for dealing with violators of international principles. Yet some things can be done to control transfer pricing and to change tax laws governing corporations. We can strengthen the bargaining power of Third World nations through sharing information and helping them build up their own economies. We can affirm the right of regulation by both host countries and headquarters countries—or, if regulation is insufficient, the right to nationalize holdings within a country with fair compensation. But if we want the benefits of international economic coordination without the losses of acquisitive private control, there is no long-run substitute for the development of a new system of international controls through international organizations such as the United Nations.

From a Christian perspective one must ask two major questions about any proposed new order: (1) What are its goals? Does it aim at justice and equal opportunity, or is it content with present forms of exploitation and inequality? (2) At whose expense and for whose benefit is it constructed? Another way of putting this is: Who casts the votes determining policies? Is it the few or the many, the privileged or the total population? The alternatives sketched in this chapter do not sufficiently meet these tests.

Any program adequate to the present world will involve a more constructive and radical demand than those of communistic, fascistic, or ultra-capitalistic revolutionaries. If we mean, by revolution, rapid and basic change, then the call of ethical theory and sociological reality is for a total revolution of freedom *and* justice *and* peace. Not any one or two of these alone will do. There is a more radical demand in the Gospel of Mark than in the gospel of Marx. To communistic and fascistic proposals, to extremist strategies, and to profit-motivated multinational corporations, we must reply that they are not revolutionary enough. We should be able to devise forms which avoid both political tyranny and economic exploitation. To that task we turn in the next chapters.

QUESTIONS FOR DISCUSSION
1. What widely held misconceptions of communism need to be changed? Evaluate communism from the standpoint of your Christian faith.

2. What do you see as the chief differences between communism and fascism? What fascist-type governments do you identify in the world today?

3. In our day of rapid change, when demands for justice must be quickly met, which general position on Chart 2 do you consider most desirable?

4. Do you agree with the above discussion of threats to liberty in this country today? If so, list some recent examples.

5. What do you consider to be the chief threats in the growth of multinational corporations? Their chief contributions? How do you think we might reduce the dangers?

PROJECTS FOR ACTION
1. Talk to several people about their description of communism. How accurate or how distorted do you find their opinions to be?

2. Visit such right-wing or left-wing bookstores as are available in your community. Note the kind of literature available and think about how you would refute its objectionable (propagandistic) features.

3. In current newspapers and magazines, watch for expressions similar to attitudes described above as extremist. Use these as conversation starters.

4. Arrange for a competent person to review Barnet and Müller, *Global Reach: The Power of the Multinational Corporations* (Simon and Schuster, 1974) for an appropriate church or community organization.

5. Work with your local church social action committee to provide more educational projects in the area of basic social theory and contemporary social systems.

CHAPTER 4
THE CONTOURS OF A NEW ORDER

Recall the familiar parable in which the great Lord of all the universe gathered all nations for judgment (Matthew 25:31-46). Some persons were separated out for punishment because they had not fed the hungry nor given drink to the thirsty. Then imagine one of those condemned (perhaps a lawyer accustomed to drawing up briefs) appealing his case by saying, "But, Lord, I did send a check for famine relief." Then in your fantasy the Lord might reply, "The records indeed show that you mailed one $10 check, but the records also show that you stayed home from the polls on the day an anti-foreign-assistance senator was elected. You did not raise your voice against iniquitous economic practices which took millions of dollars from the poor. I repeat, 'You did not feed the hungry.'"

This fanciful continuation of the story in Matthew 25 is quite true to the original intent. The test is meeting human need. That surely includes emergency relief. But it is even kinder, as well as more efficient, to keep people from getting hungry in the first place. Unless we eliminate root causes of widespread suffering, we are giving only a crumb instead of a meal.

Tooling up to do the full job requires some fairly complicated social and ethical analysis. This chapter may seem hard going to some of you. You will be tempted to stop reading and thinking. But remember that no significant personal growth takes place and no worthwhile social change is effected without hard work. When a Christian citizen shies away from complicated matters in economics and politics, it is just as bad as running a six-year-old son out of one's home because there will be difficulties in bringing him up to maturity. Refusal to think through complicated issues is actually saying to malnourished millions, "Go ahead and die. I'll look the other direction and pick daffodils on the other side of the road."

Let me hasten to add that this chapter will be manageable even without an extensive background. Most of us are not required to do the work of specialists in this field. But citizens in a democracy must develop enough competence to select a general policy which they will insist that elected or appointed experts shall implement.

To cover the ground more easily this chapter will consider desirable changes in economic practices within our country, and the next chapter will discuss a new economic order in international dealings. In both of these arenas the panaceas of the past easily become the fiascoes of the future—and the future is coming so fast you can hear the wind whistling around its edges.

NEW PURPOSES BEYOND THE ACQUISITIVE

Among the problems in our present economy analyzed in Chapter 2 were certain consequences of the acquisitive motive. The automatic operation of the traditional market system depended on persons acting in order to get the highest profits or wages. But this also has contributed to such results as faster resource exhaustion, more questionable products, and more likely exploitation of others.

Jesus proposed a decidedly different motivation for all life's activities. His word was, "Beware of all covetousness" (Luke 12:15) and "Whoever would be great among you must be your servant" (Matt. 20:26; Mark 10:43). In economic life we have commonly assumed that by serving self we would be led to do what also served others. Jesus stressed just the opposite. It is by losing one's life in the service of a great need that we truly find our own best interests (Matthew 16:25). The Christian doctrine of vocation calls for daily work in the spirit of "Let no one seek his own good, but the good of his neighbor" (1 Cor. 10:24).

This biblical teaching runs head on into the widespread feeling that our present population is not ethically mature enough to act altruistically. We have not sufficiently developed our capacities to love. No economy can go far beyond the continuing egoistic nature of its personnel. As motivation for economic activity we cannot rely on what does not exist.

This, however, is too quick and simple a pessimism. Psychological research shows that human motivation is complex. Less blatantly egoistic motivations are also among the drives of most people—including interests in security, creative work, social approval, and human decency and helpfulness. Studies in industrial psychology have convinced many employers that financial incentives release only a fraction of the energy of workers. A growing sense of social responsibility is emerging in a number of occupational groups. We might use the phrase "Thank God it's Monday" to remind us that many persons are happy in their work and look forward to returning to it.

Both ethical and economic imperatives are clear. We need to move as far as possible in the direction of appeals to more cooperative and altruistic motives. Already we can legislate against the most socially dangerous expressions of the more egoistic drives, as in impure foods or false advertising. We can encourage appeals to less egoistic motives. For the future, we can help persons release even more altruistic propensities. The multiplication of the number of persons sensitive to need and dedicated to service is unfinished business for society and a major assignment for the church.

This is related to an emerging new view of the purpose of life. Ours has become an overdeveloped society, materialistic to the point of hedonism. "Up" has been tied to "more," with higher status being assigned to successful accumulators of material gadgets. Now both personal disillusionment and ecological necessity are bringing some of us to see that this kind of growth for the sake of growth is the lifestyle of the cancer cell. We can learn from Kierkegaard's parable about the prosperous man riding at night in his luxurious carriage. With all its lamps lighted, it is not dark around him; but precisely because he has so much worldly light, he cannot see the stars.

We can now discover the stars only by shifting our chief preoccupation from physical and material things to social and spiritual values. Thereby we can release undeveloped human capacities and introduce a new age in history. We who have adequate incomes could more often concentrate our working hours on improving human relationships, eliminating injustice and war, and discovering the power of intimacy and love. We could employ more artists, music instructors, youth leaders, spiritual life counselors, national park rangers, and researchers in the relationship of religion to health. By concentrating less on the production of goods and more on the provision of services in social, intellectual, moral, esthetic, and spiritual realms, we could become rich far beyond the kind of luxury we now think the peak of achievement. These enlarged services would not require a heavy use of irreplaceable resources. We might learn part of what was meant by "having nothing, and yet possessing everything" (2 Cor. 6:10).

This would not mean economic stagnation. We would be paying persons to provide a different kind of service. Instead of a "no growth" economy, this would be a "new growth" economy. Any contraction in the manufacture of cosmetics or supersonic planes could be more than balanced by expansion of leadership for continuing education, neighborhood art classes, prayer retreats, and social reform movements. An individual's physical growth stops with adulthood, but greater mental and spiritual actualization can still continue. So a nation whose essential material needs have been met can continue growing in much more important areas.

DEMOCRATIC DECISION IN ECONOMIC AFFAIRS

The analysis in Chapter 2 pointed to another crucial weakness that makes our traditional economy less suitable for modern conditions. The rather completely unregulated old-style capitalism, which served us well in different days, has also developed certain deficiencies, such as serious depressions, or the inability to sustain a free market in the face of large-scale economic enterprise. Control by consumers is inadequate, and the economically powerful cast multiple ballots.

Because of such defects we have hesitantly and confusedly moved into a mixed economy, in which private enterprise is supplemented by government initiative in economic affairs. Most businesses are still privately owned and operated primarily within a free market. Where there are no serious social abuses this can be continued. Those production activities and service trades which find smallness an advantage are not likely to destroy the conditions necessary for a market economy. As even communist nations are beginning to discover, the market mechanism is still valuable for registering a wide variety of complex preferences. In our society, government activity should be reduced wherever projects have outlived their usefulness or bureaucratic jobs simply pad the payrolls. Considerable reduction in "overkill" military expenditure can probably be made without reducing necessary defense capability.

On the other hand, citizens through government will likely continue to insist on shaping general directions on matters like social security, or monetary and taxation policies to avoid inflation and depressions. We are not likely to turn over our military establishment to private enterprise, even though Kenneth Boulding has suggested that in terms of gross national product our Department of Defense is next to the largest socially-owned, planned economy in the world, second only to the total economic activity of the Soviet Union.[24] In a number of other crucial sectors of our highly interdependent society some overall planning is a necessity. This is particularly true for those sectors of economic activity that function like public utilities: food, energy, transportation, communications. A distinguished group of leaders in education, business, labor, and government recently signed a statement in which they said, "Planning is neither strange nor unfamiliar. Every individual and business plans for the years ahead. Our space program is a good example of planning. . . . Just as it would have been impossible for a man to go to the moon and back by accident, it is impossible for us to achieve our economic objectives by accident."[25] A central issue before us is whether the authors of this statement were right in asking for greater government participation in the economic process. Public debate on this issue very much needs to be informed by careful consideration of pro and con arguments like the following:

1. It is often argued that too much government economic action will *undermine individual initiative and responsibility.* It is said, for example, that taxes coerce persons into contributing to human needs, while beneficiaries of government-financed programs learn to live by the outstretched hand instead of the working arm.

On the other hand, some government programs can *provide better channels for initiative and responsibility,* as for example, by supporting public schools instead of teaching our own children, or by issuing social-security type benefits for which all have made a payment or benefits that require a willingness to work.

2. Building up vast government machinery is said to lead to the *expensive inefficiencies* of bureaucracy. Government would become so big and attempt to do so much that it would choke the system with papers in quadruplicate.

It is replied that wise government action *increases efficiency* by basing decision on a wider accumulation of data than any private unit has available, and by dealing with overall problems, like business recessions, that cannot be dealt with in any other way.

3. Some insist that centralizing so many decisions in government would necessitate a *loss of freedom.* Since the electorate could not handle so many decisions, control would fall into the hands of a small bureaucracy. Enforcement of every new government policy would extend coercion into another aspect of life. Especially as plans began to fail, governments would apply increasingly dictatorial controls.

Others with equal insistence would say that all the many decisions necessary are already being made, either by small economic elites or by inaction. Low wages and unemployment are even more coercive than minimum wage laws and public works projects. The electorate can handle general policy to be implemented by specialists responsible to the people. By allowing majorities instead of minorities to decide such matters, *freedoms are extended* into areas in which citizens previously had no voice. If we do not deal democratically with serious problems that continue to plague us, people will in desperation turn to dictatorship.

After carefully weighing these arguments, a group might conclude:
(a) On major matters where overall government action is important in

order "to promote the general welfare," we must not hesitate to provide it. (b) Certain safeguards should be built into our system to meet the chief objections to government action. These might include avoiding government controls at unnecessary points, plugging loopholes for the idle (whether among welfare recipients or among the rich), eliminating bureaucratic inefficiency at least as much as big business does, and remaining eternally vigilant about maintaining our political freedoms. We should use patterns of planning that decentralize decisions as much as possible. Local matters should be locally determined. At the same time, of course, issues like mining ocean resources or preventing war require some international authority.

AREAS FOR GOVERNMENT ACTION

Vigorous public debate rages around proposals for additional economic initiatives by democratic government. This section lists a considerable number of these. Each reader is invited to check the items he or she would personally favor. Before such an evaluation, however, there are two review topics appropriate for Christians. From previous pages, especially in Chapter 1, recall the radical impact of Christian love. We are called to nothing less than the nurture of the full capacities of every person on earth. This includes equal opportunity for the use of material resources and the fullest possible freedom from coercive limitations. We are to have special regard for the liberation of the poor from exploitation and oppression. Those of us who are among the rich of the world have a particular obligation and face an especially serious spiritual peril.

We have made a dedication to this lifestyle of love in a world also described earlier, especially in Chapter 2. Recall the extent of inequality, poverty, and misery in the United States and in the rest of the world. Past programs intended to relieve the situation have had too little effect. Progressive tax rates have not produced a significantly higher percentage of taxes from the rich. While we have given welfare to the poor, we have also given subsidies to the rich. Nor have the devices we expected to protect economic freedom worked equally well for all. Remembering our divine calling reminds us that Christians are to go beyond present arrangements and commonly accepted attitudes. To keep up in a dynamic world means continuously arriving at new conclusions that we never held before. With all this in mind, consider which of the following programs Christians should now advocate for government action.

1. One general category all of us would probably put on our lists is legislating against acts that would allow the few to exploit the many.

For this reason we support a criminal code on the law books. We are coming to accept legislation to safeguard against racist and sexist discrimination. Should we now also become more enthusiastic about protections against class discrimination? We are just beginning to act more effectively against disproportionate political influence by the wealthy, as in campaign contributions or local financing of superior public schools in affluent neighborhoods while the ghettos go begging. Can we move toward greater equality of opportunity without serious tax reform designed to close loopholes and preferential treatment, and to become more steeply progressive in its impact? At the other end of the economic scale, should we provide more of those services which are of greater help to the poor than to the rich—such as education, parks, low-cost housing, and public transportation? For those willing and able to work, should there be a floor for incomes, high enough to provide the essentials of a decent life and below which we would allow no one to fall? By a very high tax rate in the upper brackets, should we also establish a wealth-accumulation ceiling beyond which no one could go? What do you suppose the Old Testament prophets and Jesus would say about this? Consider their socioeconomic attitudes as recorded in the Bible, in contrast to the way we have sometimes rationalized those sayings to our own comfort.

2. Another source of exploitation is unregulated monopoly. The potential seriousness of this has been pointed out in the earlier discussion of multinational corporations. No private economic organization should be allowed to override the will of the people expressed through government. We have provided some protections in anti-trust laws and in commission regulation of those monopolies we allow, such as telephone or electric power companies. We have not, however, prevented the growth of gigantic centers of economic power. We have been reluctant to "bust the trusts" because we wanted their efficiency in some types of business even while we did not like their power over prices. There were also difficulties with regulation—the expense of getting full, accurate information, the difficulty of dealing with their political and economic resourcefulness, the limitations of negative control as over against original, positive decision-making.

When fragmentation and regulation fail, there is a strong argument for socializing basic enterprises that should function in a coordinated way. This is no panacea, and public corporations should not control too much of the economy. But neither is there any particular reason that socially-owned parks and bus companies should be considered in the American tradition while socially-owned grocery stores and oil refineries are labeled un-American. Rail and air transportation is at least as essential a public service as is flood control or street maintenance. If we believe that the earth is the Lord's and that all God's children are to have access to its bounty, there is nothing wrong with social ownership as such. Nations have had good experiences and bad experiences with it. Our best approach is not doctrinaire, but pragmatic. The question is to determine *where* social ownership is an appropriate solution. If we develop a tradition of dedicated and efficient civil service, we are likely to be somewhat more often impressed with the social ownership alternative. As the pressure toward gigantic corporations continues, we will be driven either to socialization or to much stricter regulation.

3. Government action is also often the most effective way to reach social goals that can be accomplished only if we all act together. There are obvious advantages in a single system of water mains or highways. Control of inflation, or of cycles of prosperity and depression, is impossible without some joint action in things like monetary and fiscal policy, tax rates, and public works programs. Such avoidance of deep depressions as we have accomplished is due to the widespread acceptance, by all major political parties, of this kind of national action. Protection of natural resources is not possible if only some persons are restrained from raping the forests. This is a matter of everybody being regulated or no one getting the benefit. A rational energy policy still demands more common action. We cannot expect one manufacturer to install costly equipment for pollution control, if his competitors can get by without it and thereby undersell the conscientious producer.

4. Another group of economic activities is too expensive or risky for private enterprise, or returns no commensurate profit and therefore does not attract private investors. Illustrations are river and harbor improvement, basic educational systems, space explorations, or the development of solar energy. Protection against lethal pollution will require much more mass transportation. Because such transportation often cannot be operated without loss, governments must at least share the job. Citizens will pay for clean air through taxes, even as they paid for highways.

5. With strong majority support we use certain social measures to protect ourselves against major economic hazards which may strike any one of us and usually through no fault of our own. The usual illustrations are unemployment, old age, death of the breadwinner, industrial accidents, sickness, and crop failure. Risks such as these can be pooled through some approximation to an insurance plan. When the risks are universal and there are advantages in a single

system, or when the uncertainties are so great that private insurance finds coverage difficult, nations have quite understandably turned to government provisions. Various social security systems cover most of the hazards on this list. In the United States the chief exception, at the moment, is sickness. If we follow our other precedents, as well as the lead of other industrial nations, we are likely to incorporate this also into some sort of overall plan for the entire nation. For new expressions of justice and human concern should other individual, undeserved losses be shared by reimbursing victims of crime, war, or major natural disasters like earthquakes?

6. One of the most promising and exciting possibilities beginning to appear is the new lifestyle discussed earlier in this chapter as potentially a new stage in civilization. This is the possibility of placing less emphasis on the production and use of material luxuries, and investing much more energy in the achievement of higher social and spiritual values. The transition to such a new era in history cannot come without important activity by government. At the moment, we still depend on increases in the old types of demand to pull us out of recessions and to provide full employment without inflation. The shift to meeting a new type of demand will be as difficult as moving from a war-production to a peace-production economy. Manufacturing for the needs of poor nations and providing services like environmental enhancement, extended educational opportunities, widespread resources in the arts, and more activists working on social reform will require seed money. The transition will require planning and coordination. This may turn out to be the greatest service government can render in the years ahead.

The general question before us is no longer government intervention as part of a mixed economy. That has already been accepted. The question now is how much intervention and for whose interests. Will we now move with resolution toward more equal opportunity for the disadvantaged, a more widespread freedom of participation, a new quality of life? In the long run this would provide greater fulfillment both for those who are now rich and for those who are now poor. On the other hand, if we continue our traditional stress on material accumulation and unregulated private profit seeking, there is no way of avoiding economic and environmental collapse, and worldwide revolution against present inequities. We may have a great new future on the basis of a decidedly different and more Christian approach. Will Christians give leadership in making drastic enough changes to solve deep-seated problems? Or will we attempt to make do with mild, palliative reforms that actually strengthen those aspects of the system which cause the problems? As Dag Hammarskjöld put it, "It is when we all play safe that we create a world of utmost insecurity." In matters of economic justice, when there are rapidly approaching deadlines attached, we must carefully plan and energetically take whatever big leaps are called for. It is impossible to cross a chasm in two small jumps.

QUESTIONS FOR DISCUSSION
1. Allen Hunter has suggested that our motives are not only mixed, but that they are homogenized. List the variety of motives that lead you to work. What would it take to make your own action more altruistic?
  2. What more do you think we could do as a people to strengthen the service motive in economic life? What could the church do?
  3. What possibilities do you see for a national lifestyle that would emphasize higher types of values? What next steps might be taken? Initial advice is available from your denomination's hunger program coordinator.
  4. Analyze the above pro and con arguments concerning the extension of government economic initiative. What is your own position on each of the contrasting sets of arguments? What others would you suggest?
  5. Review the biblical criteria discussed in Chapter 1. Relate these criteria to the areas for possible government action discussed in this chapter. In the light of Christian insight would you add to or subtract from this list?

PROJECTS FOR ACTION
1. Conversation and correspondence are important ways to form public opinion. In your own conversation and correspondence watch for opportunities to share your class discussion or your personal opinion on some of these matters.
  2. In some countries consumers' cooperatives very effectively play a larger part in a mixed economy than they do in the United States. If there is a bona fide cooperative in your area controlled by consumers, arrange a visit. Some small, emergency co-ops have recently organized to meet inflation in food prices. One in your area may need help. Or write the Cooperative League of the U.S.A. (1828 L St., N.W., Washington, D.C. 20036) for material on larger, well-established cooperatives.
  3. Find out where the major political parties and your present representatives in Congress stand on those issues discussed above which seem most important to you. Also correspond with your denomi-

nation's Church and Society department to ascertain church policy statements on these issues. What does this say about your keeping in touch with your representatives as issues become timely? What does this suggest about your party affiliation or preference?

4. Arrange a workshop on the future structure of the economy with interested persons from your class or church and two teachers of economics who hold different opinions. Keep Christian criteria prominent in the discussion. If a significant consensus emerges, give publicity to it.

5. Organize groups in which lay persons can share and explore together the ethical dilemmas and opportunities they face on their jobs. How can they help each other improve economic practices?

6. Obtain and use the study/action kit, *Metamorphosis: Christians Choosing Lifestyles for a World in Crisis*, a Doing the Word Resource Kit (John Knox Press, 1976), $15. Order from your denominational curriculum order department.

CHAPTER 5
A NEW ECONOMY FOR THE WORLD

If we search hard enough for them, two symbols of our aspirations rise against the Manhattan skyline. The Statue of Liberty speaks of what is best in the American intention. With the promise of freedom and opportunity, it welcomes to these shores the dispossessed of the earth. Then farther within the labyrinth of the city, the United Nations building announces that all nations must now cooperate to deliver that promise together. Both symbols, however, are dwarfed by skyscrapers predominantly filled with enterprises promoting our own national interests and creature comforts. Neither the sharing of resources with others, nor even hospitality for cooperative self-help, are actual priority concerns. One has to have a particular location and perspective to see the Statue of Liberty and the United Nations building at all.

The perspective of Christian faith would clarify the need for innovations not only in the national, but also in the international economic order. Christians hope for a united humanity cooperatively providing full opportunity for every person. Christians seek the abolition of misery and injustice, and the provision of global freedom and dignity. Abraham Lincoln saw that a nation cannot continue half slave and half free; we should see that the world cannot be preserved half stuffed and half starved.

INESCAPABLE REALITIES
Remember the words of the prophets promising doom for those who "trample upon the poor," and the New Testament picture of punishment for those who do not feed the hungry. Then look at a sampler of statistics describing our world. Nine hundred million people subsist with cash incomes of less than $75 a year, under conditions that World Bank President Robert McNamara has called "so deprived as to be below any rational definition of human decency."[26] Those acutely hungry in the world number about 460 million. If we add those who lack essential nutrients in their diet (and therefore cannot function at

full capacity), the number rises to between one and two billion, as estimated by the United Nations Food and Agriculture Organization.[27]

What this means is suggested by the experience of one Peace Corps worker. At first he was outraged by the apparent laziness of those in a remote village in Ecuador. Then circumstances forced him to exist on their diet. He quickly learned why so many of the world's farmers can work only a few hours a day. As he put it, "There are just so many miles to a gallon of bananas."[28] In most of the world the major nutritional problem is malnutrition. Our number one nutritional problem is obesity; 40 percent of Americans are overweight, according to the *American Medical Association Journal* (July 13, 1970).

From 1972 to 1974, according to the Overseas Development Council, the average annual per capita grain consumption (both directly and indirectly in meat, eggs, and milk) was 1,850 pounds for the United States and about 400 pounds for the developing countries. A group of environmental scientists estimated that a person in the United States during the course of a lifetime would consume at least 20 times as much as a typical person in India, while contributing about 50 times as much pollution to the environment. In 1970 the average per capita consumption of fossil fuels in the developed countries was 4,420 kilograms in comparison with 246 for the developing countries. Corresponding figures for steel were 480 and 44. About 6 percent of the world's population (in the United States) consume about 40 percent of the world's production of natural resources. Gandhi has often been quoted as saying that the world has enough for everyone's need, but not for everyone's greed.

Some persons in the developing world share the responsibility for this situation. Some leaders in poorer nations have perpetrated injustices on their own people. Some prevailing popular habits do keep living standards lower. But there are other major causes that the developing nations can do very little about. We inherited a head start from the work of our ancestors, along with important natural and political advantages. This combination cannot be duplicated by the "have not" nations. We have no right to tell them "Do it the way we did."

We have a heavy responsibility for the condition of the developing nations because our prosperity has to a great extent depended upon their poverty. The Bible insists, "Love does no wrong to a neighbor" (Rom. 13:10). Yet our living standard is higher partly because it was built on low wages and low selling prices in the mines and plantations of the Third World. Developing countries that produce oil, copper, and other resources are finally beginning to do what we have been doing for a long time—namely, raise prices to the highest point demand will allow, in order to gain the maximum profit. We may not like being called "exploiter" or "oppressor" by leaders of the Third World. Yet in a world of limited resources it is indubitably true that one person's wealth becomes another person's poverty. When there is not enough to go around, what I have another person cannot have. The current "affluence explosion" among the middle and upper classes in our part of the world is using up resources that could be directed to greater human needs.

By simply maintaining our own standard of living, we "load men with intolerable burdens, and will not put a single finger to the load" (Luke 11:46, NEB). These words of Jesus were directed with broader meaning to very prestigious religious leaders in Israel. We can apply them to the economic situation and to those widely regarded among us as most moral and successful. If this continues, since God is just, it it only a question of time until the word of Amos comes true and all our feasts will be turned into funerals, and all our songs into lamentations (Amos 8:10).

An additional heavy responsibility is that we have not found an alternative to war or massive armaments. By our military assistance funds and arms sales we have even encouraged poor nations to maintain a high level of military expenditure, instead of using these resources for other desperate needs. This general situation is getting worse instead of better. Expressed in constant 1972 dollars, world arms expenditures rose from $197 billion in 1963 to $241 billion in 1973.[29] Global military costs are now considerably larger than the total income of the poorer half of the world. In a single day the United States spends more for current military purposes than a full year's budget of the UN World Food Program. "It takes the Department of Defense a mere 29 hours to consume what the UN Development Program uses in a year."[30] Sen. Mark O. Hatfield recently pointed out that for each dollar the United States spends "to alleviate suffering and enhance human life throughout the world, we spend $50.00 for the weapons and forces geared to the destruction of life."[31]

In a similar vein cartoonist Frank Miller shows Uncle Sam assuring a group of Third World countries, "Sure you need food, clothes and hospitals. All of that will take time. What you need right now is a modern weapons system—guns, jets, rockets. . . ." Probably the greatest economic contribution we could make to alleviate world suffering would be the prevention of war and the elimination of the crushing world burden of armaments. Soon after leaving his military career to become President, Dwight D. Eisenhower said, "Every gun that is made, every warship launched, every rocket fired signifies, in the final sense, a theft from those who hunger and are not fed, those who are cold and are not clothed."[32]

Because of the awakening of the Third World, never before have so many wanted so much. Because they also see possible ways to gain it, we are now in a tense revolutionary situation. We cannot postpone the poor. They are here. They are turbulent. They are an inescapable ethical stimulus. We may try by superior force to suppress the developing nations, in an effort to keep them quietly poor. Thus we would imitate the totalitarian methods we criticize, and our policy would only lead to a greater explosion. As Norman Cousins once said, "History is a vast early-warning system." The consequences of enforced injustice have been abundantly demonstrated. That leaves open to us only the policy of becoming staunch allies of the Third and Fourth Worlds in accelerating their liberation by whatever arrangements are most just and effective.

NEW DIMENSIONS FOR SHARING

So long as we do not work against vast worldwide inequality, others will continue to die physically through malnutrition while we continue to die spiritually through callous insensitivity. So hard is it for the rich to enter the kingdom of heaven. There is no redemption apart from repentance. There is no salvation, theologically or economically, apart from sharing more extensively than ever before in history.

The necessary ethical response is related to certain cold hard facts of economic life. There can be no adequate raising of standards of living for the developing world without sufficient capital to pay for whatever equipment is necessary to increase productivity. Furthermore, a sufficient response from more fortunate nations will have to come partially from government funds. Personal philanthropy is not enough for the need. Private investment by business firms is not attracted to some of the basic needs that do not return a profit, such as schools or highways. In addition, there is understandable resistance by developing nations to having large sections of their economies controlled by outside corporations.

The suggestion that we increase our government appropriations for development assistance programs immediately arouses a number of arguments for and against. In favor of such an increase is (1) the dismal condition of masses of people through no fault of their own. This argument is reinforced by the kind of economic analysis just referred to. (2) More adequate assistance for more rapid development could also contribute to international understanding and world peace, since it would relieve a major source of tension and conflict. (3) It can also be argued that aid stimulates world trade and helps United States business by providing more customers for our products.

Typical arguments against economic assistance include: (1) the possibility that by large gifts we "kill the goose that lays the golden egg." There obviously needs to be a limit somewhere. We could not maintain our ability to contribute if we gave away a substantial part of our productive capacity. But we are nowhere near that limit. Producing for world needs can also stimulate appropriate industry, increasing the quality of life available to us. (2) Some fear that raising standards of living will speed up population increase in the developing world. Certainly help in population control is an important part of any comprehensive aid package. But population growth is generated by poverty. There is evidence also that rising living standards contribute to lower birth rates, since (a) there is less social pressure for a large number of children to guarantee their survival to adulthood and to provide for parents in old age, and (b) other interests and sources for self-fulfillment become available, especially for women.

(3) Other common objections directed against government aid are not arguments against aid as such, but only against particular types of programs. Thirty years of experience with "foreign aid" has taught administrators of development assistance that the criteria for aid are as important as the amount paid. The conditions for aid should include safeguards against the degree of paternalism which becomes demoralizing, or against the irresponsible use of funds, or against the diversion of funds in profits to the rich instead of benefits to the poor. Aid can be curtailed if funds are not used for the purposes originally agreed upon. Considerations such as these suggest improvements in types of aid rather than the elimination of aid.

Careful group analysis of such pro and con arguments often leads to a consensus drawing on the most defensible observations by both sides. When basic facts are presented, Christians are likely to be impressed by human need and by the importance of larger aid and trade for a more cooperative and peaceful world. Therefore, part of the consensus position becomes increased economic assistance. At the same time, observations about past defects lead to demands for a greatly reformed program.

Desirable reforms might include (1) concentration on the real needs of developing nations rather than grossly distorting programs to fit our own economic needs or political interests; (2) preference to countries that are both needy and responsible in their approach to development (including land and income reforms to reduce inequality, all possible extensions of human rights, restraint in military spending, and constructive use of previous funds); (3) separate classification of military assistance, lest it give us a false picture of the amount of economic assistance we are providing; (4) administration of a higher percentage of our funds by international agencies, which by joint participation can reduce paternalism and at the same time more easily impose conditions for continued aid.

By such reforms we can provide better assistance. We can also give more. The picture of the United States as the world's Santa Claus does not survive comprehensive statistics. Our official contributions for development assistance, as a percentage of gross national product, in 1974 ranked us fourteenth among the seventeen industrialized members of the Development Assistance Committee of the Organization for Economic Cooperation and Development. (See Chart 3.) Our percentage figure was less than half that of countries like Sweden, the Netherlands, France, and Canada. While we contributed a larger amount of money, the significant figure is the percentage of our total production, out of which the contribution is made. We would scarcely consider that a million-dollar-a-year man had done his duty by the church with a contribution of $1,000 if a person with a $50,000 income was giving $500. We really cannot delete from the Bible the statement, "Every one to whom much is given, of him will much be required" (Luke 12:48).

NEW ARRANGEMENTS FOR JUSTICE

Kurt Waldheim, Secretary General of the United Nations, has pointed out that delivering nations from economic, as well as political, dependency requires going beyond economic aid to a new international economic order. He wrote, "The international system of economic and trade relations which was devised 30 years ago is now manifestly inadequate for the needs of the world community as a whole. The charge against that order in the past was that it worked well for the affluent and against the poor. It cannot now even be said that it works well for the affluent."[33]

In immediate economic results (though not in long-run social and spiritual consequences) present arrangements favor the rich and powerful nations. Countries of widely differing economic strength do not do business as equals. Developed nations have many bargaining advantages. Developing nations charge with considerable accuracy that world monetary and trade policies are established for the benefit of industrialized countries. The natural resources of developing nations have been exploited with minimal benefit to themselves. The

Chart 3
1974 ASSISTANCE AS PERCENTAGE OF GNP

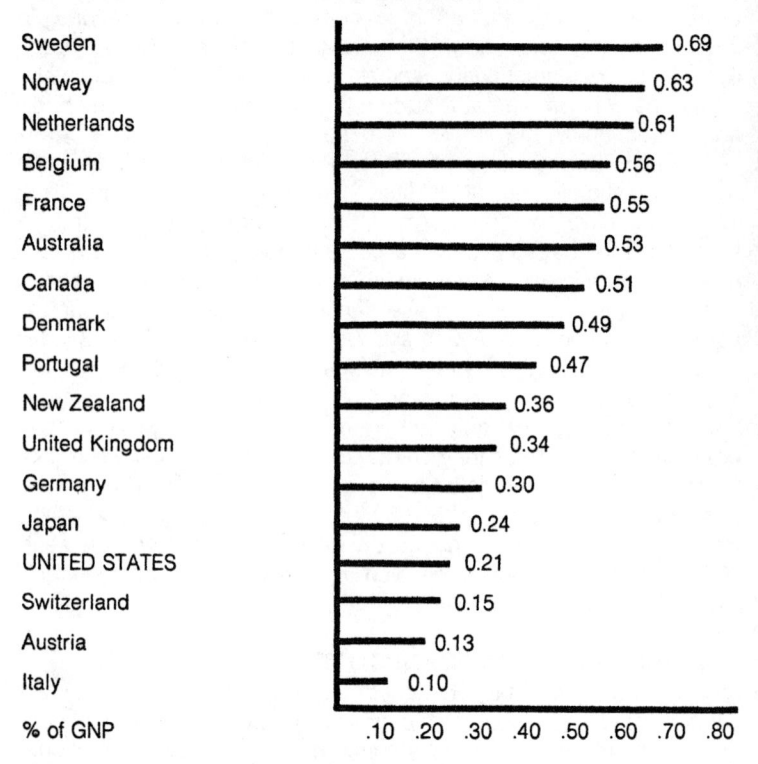

Country	% of GNP
Sweden	0.69
Norway	0.63
Netherlands	0.61
Belgium	0.56
France	0.55
Australia	0.53
Canada	0.51
Denmark	0.49
Portugal	0.47
New Zealand	0.36
United Kingdom	0.34
Germany	0.30
Japan	0.24
UNITED STATES	0.21
Switzerland	0.15
Austria	0.13
Italy	0.10

Estimate of official development assistance. Source: Organization for Economic Cooperation and Development.

economies of developing nations have been shaped to service the needs of developed nations. The chief exports of the developing world, raw materials and primary products, are subject to serious price fluctuations. Their infant manufacturing industries are restricted in growth because they cannot export through the tariff walls of the developed world. All these things make it easier for the rich to grow richer, and make it harder to close the inequality gap between rich and poor.

Developing countries also have little power to change existing arrangements, since decision-making power is largely in the hands of those who already have wealth and power. There seems to be little hope unless the industrialized nations can come to see, as Kurt Waldheim suggested, that what was most profitable for them in the past is no longer in their long-run best interest, and that by continuation of present policies they can only reap a bitter harvest. A significant redistribution of wealth and power becomes now not only a matter of justice but also of self-interest.

A continuation of arrangements that exploit the weak is quite contradictory to the considerate and cooperative human relationships that Christians seek. Isaiah's picture of God's intention included, "They shall not hurt or destroy in all my holy mountain" (Isa. 11:9; 65:25). The New Testament compares fellowship within the church to the parts of the body. No part can reject the others. The eye cannot deny its need of the hand, nor the head of the feet. The recognition of this kind of relationship we also desire for the world. On a worldwide scale we would have persons increasingly recognize that "if one member suffers, all suffer together; if one member is honored, all rejoice together" (1 Cor. 12:26). Some aspects of present competitiveness invite us to do just the opposite: to rejoice at another's failure, and to be saddened by another's success.

Even on grounds of simple decency, the unfair rules of the game must be changed. The successful have no right to block the successes of others. When only those over six feet tall are allowed to shoot at the basket, those under six feet will not have a good scoring record. It becomes even worse when short players are required to feed the ball to tall stars, and when a salary is paid only to those who shoot the goals. Akporode Clark, Nigerian representative to the United Nations Conference on Trade and Development, pointed out that the flow of economic "aid" to developing countries has been more than balanced by the flow of assistance to rich countries because of underpricing of commodities they bought from poorer nations. He added, "The developing countries cannot continue to aid the developed countries to live above their means."[34]

In recent international negotiation, as at regular and special sessions of the United Nations Assembly in 1974 and 1975, developing nations have been asking for higher and more stable prices for the commodities they are able to export, such as copper, bauxite, coffee, or cocoa. This kind of trade would also provide important aid to their development. A drop in the price of coffee, for example, can wipe out the effect of our government assistance funds to coffee-producing countries. The effect is particularly devastating if a drop in the price of exported raw materials coincides with an inflationary rise in prices of manufactured goods which developing nations must import.

Better prices for the primary products which developing nations have to sell might be gained by international stockpiles or by compensatory financing if export earnings drop. If some such international measures do not succeed, more developing countries will try to form the kind of joint marketing associations which have so rapidly raised the price of oil.

The poorer nations could also earn higher incomes if they processed some of their primary commodities within their own country and exported the finished product. There is often more help for poverty in selling shirts than in exporting cotton, or in shipping steel instead of iron ore. Developing nations therefore ask for such tariff adjustments as will allow them to sell those finished products which they can advantageously produce. Depending on the conditions of the particular industry, this might require within industrialized nations a transition to producing the kinds of goods or services they can even more advantageously provide. Economists point out that in the long run we would all be better off for this kind of international division of labor, giving everyone a fair chance at a decent standard of living.

Developing countries are also asking for increased participation in decision-making on matters which vitally affect them. They feel, for example, that agencies supplying international development funds are dominated by the rich creditor nations. Also, they ask for more effective participation in the control of those powerful multinational corporations which in 1970 accounted for one sixth of world production, including 40 percent of world industrial production.[35] This percentage, of course, is increasing. These corporations do not bring as much capital into developing countries as we often think. Much of their capital comes from profits within the developing country, or in borrowing from its banks (which leaves less capital for local enterprises). By their advertising, multinationals may encourage consumption of luxury goods which are not needed. It is cheaper for "cosmocorps" to introduce technology already developed in industrialized nations. This technology may be excessively capital-intensive in situations where a more labor-intensive technology would be more appropriate. In all these ways multinational corporations, motivated by a desire for maximum profits for foreign stockholders, may actually impede the development of poorer nations.[36] Through an international code of conduct and through their own laws, developing countries deserve the power to control foreign corporations in order to protect their domestic freedoms, and their economic and social aims.

At the Seventh Special Session of the United Nations Assembly, the United States did indicate increasing support for the general aims of the developing nations in designing new international procedures. As Secretary of State Henry Kissinger put it, "We have heard your voices. We embrace your hopes. We will join in your efforts." The years ahead will indicate how much of this was rhetoric and how much was serious intention. Expressions of public support for justice in economic policies will influence the outcome. If we avoid foot-dragging, our support may result in at least as great a watershed in world history as was the initial introduction of the Marshall Plan to aid European recovery after World War II.

FUNDAMENTAL CHANGES IN SYSTEMS

Chapters 2 and 4 included a discussion of weaknesses in our traditional economy which led us into our present mixed system. We continue to discover necessary improvements in our mix. Developing nations face a similar dilemma regarding what to preserve and what to change in their own economies. It is understandable that different countries in somewhat differing circumstances should try different combinations. From the standpoint of world progress, it is even desirable that there should be somewhat differing experiments in various countries. All of us can then learn from each other's experiences.

In our reluctance to accept novel systems in the developing world we have often been quite self-contradictory. We criticize poorer nations for not getting aid funds to the poor. Relieving the misery of the masses would often require basic political and economic changes to shift power from the traditionally privileged to the poor and powerless. But then we also insist that developing countries keep the established system which promotes the very inequities to which we object.

All too often economic aid has been a subsidy to repressive regimes which obstruct necessary reforms. Effective use of assistance funds requires thoroughgoing social changes like land and tax reform, anticorruption measures, economic planning, and public control of resources. We need to look more kindly upon those groups working for such basic changes, instead of placing obstacles in their path. Our own highest ideals should lead us in this sense to become the allies of responsible revolution instead of the protectors of the evils of the past.

We might well withhold aid from the most oppressive and reactionary regimes, whether leftist or rightist. But we ought not discriminate against countries within a wide range of systems between those extremes. We might well understand that developing nations need more authoritarian regimes until they have achieved the educational and equalitarian resources for democracy, but we should favor regimes with a genuine commitment to the extension of liberty as soon as that becomes possible. We ought not, however, reduce assistance to nations which prefer a neutralist foreign policy as between the Eastern and Western blocs, nor to those nations which incorporate into their mixed domestic economy large measures of socialization.

We aid other nations not only by assistance funds or encouraging reform, but also by providing an example of rapid, peaceful, and basic improvement. Our own system can embody greater concern for the needs of the poor and fuller extensions of liberty to all. We can go farther in sharply reducing inequalities in wealth and opportunity, and in eliminating the dominating influence of great centers of economic power in the United States. We can more adequately support international action for peace and justice. Then we would less often find ourselves preaching to others what we do not practice ourselves.

This might well be the time to review the first part of Chapter 1, which elaborated the Christian thrust toward the new and the better. It is the purpose of God to make all things new. The burden of proof is on any presently existing situation. The book of Isaiah describes God as busy creating a situation where there will not be "weeping and the cry of distress." There will be a new order in which "the former things shall not be remembered or come into mind" (Isa. 65:17-19). According to Isaiah, human rejection of the new order brings the devastating consequences of rebellion against God. Yet God remains always ready to act through persons. "I was ready to be sought by those who did not ask for me; I was ready to be found by those who did not seek me" (Isa. 65:1). How do these tragic words apply to us?

QUESTIONS FOR DISCUSSION
1. To persons in Tanzania or the Sahel who are slowly starving, in what sense may we speak convincingly of the earth being filled with the glory of God?

2. Arnold Toynbee has been quoted as saying, "Our age will be remembered not for its horrifying crimes or its astonishing inventions but because it is the first generation since the dawn of history in which humankind dared to believe it practical to make the benefits of civilization available to the whole human race." In the light of the content of this chapter, summarize what needs to be done to actualize this hope.

3. In view of statistics on world inequality presented in this chapter, do we as a nation have a right to spend billions of dollars on armaments and comparative pennies on economic assistance to poor nations? Might we be just as safe militarily with somewhat lower arms expenditures and with the world harboring less discontent and turmoil

due to poverty? How would you reduce military expenditures, or to what ends might military facilities in your region be diverted?

4. Role play a congressional debate on increasing economic assistance appropriations, using and adding to the pro and con arguments suggested in this chapter. Or role play a bargaining session over terms of trade between a coffee-producing country, like El Salvador, and the United States. (Details available in Thomas Fenton, *Coffee, the Rules of the Game, and You.* Revised edition available from The Christophers, 12 E. 48th Street, New York, N.Y. 10017, $2 per hundred.)

5. In what ways do we need to go beyond charity to justice? In the light of the Christian emphasis on brotherhood and sisterhood, are the developing nations justified in asking for changes in the international economic order of the sort discussed in the section on "New Arrangements for Justice"?

6. What reforms would you suggest in the economic and political systems of (a) the developing nations and (b) our own nation if it is to become a more convincing example?

PROJECTS FOR ACTION

1. Prepare a worship service on this general theme for your congregation or for an interdenominational event. You might use "Iracema's Story" in *The Christian Century,* November 12, 1975, pp. 1024-31.

2. From a file of church bulletins, classify sermon subjects for the last three to six months. Has there been a sermon in this area? If not, ask the minister to preach on this subject. Do a similar thing for the topics of courses which have been offered in youth and adult church school classes. Plan an event to expose your whole congregation to the issues.

3. Churches have engaged in economic assistance for a long time. Missionary schools, hospitals, and similar agencies have contributed to the infrastructure essential to economic development. Investigate which projects are currently most relevant in your denomination's overseas program, and secure larger contributions from your congregation (including yourself).

4. Write or interview your congressional representatives on bills now pending on economic assistance or changes in international economic practices. Two public policy networks that deal with such issues are:

(a) IMPACT, an interreligious agency sponsored by twenty national religious agencies, which provides timely information on issues before Congress. Send your name, address, telephone, denomination, and Congressional Representative's name, plus $5 annual membership fee to IMPACT, 110 Maryland Ave., N.E., Washington, D.C. 20002.

(b) BREAD FOR THE WORLD, a Christian citizens' movement concerned about policy issues that affect hungry people. For a monthly newsletter and other assistance, send name, address, phone number, and the name of your Congressional Representative. along with $10 annual membership fee to BREAD FOR THE WORLD, 235 East 49th Street. New York. N.Y. 10017.

5. Public opinion on issues of aid and trade has been deeply infected by numerous rationalizations attempting to justify our niggardliness. Whenever in conversation you hear such a false "justification," reply immediately, denying distortions and cutting through the rationalization with a positive Christian concern for suffering. Always with appreciation for the opponent as person, nevertheless make it clear that a large percentage of the public is no longer willing to "buy" outmoded defenses of selfishness. Helen Keller suggested that as we are now waking up to the imperfections of our social structures, "This is not a time. . . . of timid beginnings that steal into life with soft apologies and dainty grace. It is a time for loud-voiced, open speech and fearless thinking . . . , a time for all that is robust and vehement and bold."

CHAPTER 6
CONSTRUCTIVE ACTION BY CHRISTIANS

Imagine a fireplace, you and your spouse or best friend at a richly set table for two, candlelight, steak, apple pie, and whatever else you would add to your personal recipe for pleasure. Then add one other element to your fantasy. Your brother and sister are lying on beds in the next room, starving. Could you eat?

"A Declaration of Evangelical Social Concern," signed by a group of evangelical leaders in Chicago in 1973, said, "Before God and a billion hungry neighbors, we must rethink our values. . . ." The billion hungry neighbors are in the next room of this tiny spaceship earth. And if we acted "before God," really doing the will of God, then we would be able to think of God doing what we are doing. Can we without consternation imagine God saying what we are saying, doing what we are doing, eating what we are eating?

Or to put this another way, if we habitually did not show up for birthday parties for our children, or missed crucial business appointments on which the life of our company depended, simply because we preferred to watch television in a nearby motel, we would consider this monstrous. If we then do not show up for participation in social struggle where God expects us to be, is not that even more monstrous? In this book we have spoken of world need, the plan of God, the inadequacies of existing systems, and desirable new directions for our nation and the world. What is the life response to which God now calls each of us?

AN UNCOMMON RENOVATION OF ATTITUDES
A first requirement is a major shift in attitudes which would set us in opposition to some basic elements in our culture. To be sure, Christians see this theoretical point in general terms; but few among us have taken it seriously enough to live much differently. Jesus was so insistent on a new way of life that he harshly condemned scribes and Pharisees whom others would have placed among the "best" people of his day. The equivalent today might be to denounce ministers and

professors of New Testament as blind leaders of the blind. (See Matthew 15:14.)

The Christian revolution is total, rebuilding every aspect of life, and it is continuous and unending. We never fully obtain the goals of God. It is always accurate to say, "Not that I have already obtained this or am already perfect; but I press on . . ." (Phil. 3:12). We are now confronted with nothing less than a series of basic choices about the purposes of our existence. Unless we make such decisions in the light of the full implications of our theological position, our changes are likely to be trivial.

1. One direction for attitude change by the Christian is from primary concern for self to major concern for the peoples of the world. This means that we can no longer be content with simply going about our ordinary business. Searching for God's viewpoint injects us into the world with eyes that see and ears that hear the suffering and the hurt, instead of remaining closed to what is too painful or threatening. The problems of rejected persons become our problems and their gains become our gains.

We would condemn the person who demanded extra space in a lifeboat in order to be able to lie down and rest while others were still drowning in the sea. Until our consciences are aroused, we remain unaware that this is just what we in the industrialized world are doing—enjoying more than our share while others lack the means of life. In fact, we behave like the privileged few in first-class accommodations, while the mass of humanity lacks basic provisions. In our sub-Christian culture some of us even give special honor to the person who takes up most space in the lifeboat by spending the most wealth for his or her personal use.

2. Another trajectory of movement is from acting on the basis of immediate wants to taking future generations more seriously into account. It seems particularly hard for our generation to sacrifice something we want right now for the sake of future values. For many persons credit cards and unbalanced budgets indicate an inability to endure temporary inconvenience. As we face greater scarcities of raw materials and growing accumulation of pollution, we need the long-distance vision of those who comprehend Jesus' announcement of the kingdom of God.

3. Christians move from thoughtless indulgence in material things to a remembrance that our first loyalty is to higher values. When we seek first the kingdom of God (Matthew 6:33), we become mightily concerned about social improvement and spiritual growth. We resist

the pressure of the mass media, which often teach us that a person's life *does* consist in the abundance of possessions. (For the biblical teaching, cf. Luke 12:15.) We surrender to the popular notion that the only acceptable direction for wages and profits is up. The incomes of plumbers or professionals or industrialists can become too high. Prices are then driven up to the point that the poor cannot buy and our businesses cannot meet foreign competition. At the same time, those receiving higher incomes spend too much on wasteful luxuries which tragically exhaust resources.

There are times when the quest for more of a single value equals less of many other values. Increasing the dosage of medicine may be curative up to a point. Beyond that point further increases become poisonous. So it is with private incomes and material possessions.

4. Another necessary shift in popular morality would be to replace a predatory, or even an apathetic, lifestyle by substituting active concern and continuous creativity. Well-intentioned people who do nothing actually weaken the forces of righteousness. By sins of omission they strengthen the opposition, making it more likely that the forces of evil will win. It is not enough to be a conventionally passive citizen with a decent home and no police record. As Thoreau once observed, "So we defend ourselves and our hen-roosts, and maintain slavery." Obadiah (vs. 11) likewise said, "On the day that you stood aloof, . . . you were like one of them" (that is, the looters of Jerusalem). Our religious heritage teaches that life is not so much lost by dying physically, as by living without awareness and action. Those who never express that kind of dedication will end their lives without ever beginning them.

CHANGES IN PERSONAL AND FAMILY LIFESTYLES

Under present world conditions, can we conscientiously spend as much on ourselves as we have considered normal in our affluent society? Except for a few obviously lethal items, we commonly assume that it is morally acceptable to buy whatever we can afford. Now we are recognizing the limited resources of the earth. It is becoming increasingly clear that if we continue to maintain the same material standard of living we have had in the past, we will condemn others to starvation. This is as certain a source of death as is shooting. Under present world conditions, much consumer demand in industrialized countries is immoral. In 1973 our government disbursements for foreign economic aid were about $3 billion. Meanwhile we in the United States were spending $7.8 billion for toilet articles and preparations, $13.6 billion for tobacco products, and $21.5 billion for alcoholic beverages. (See Chart 4.) What does the principle of the cross mean in a Cadillac culture?

When a washing preparation gets clothes clean and white, why perfect a new one that gets clothes cleaner than clean and whiter than white? Those soft drinks that are mostly water and sugar, like those breakfast cereals that are largely sugar and air, are health hazards as well as resource wasters. We are seduced by irresponsible advertising into suicidal consumer patterns. They are suicidal both because of the dangers in highly processed products and in worldwide revolution against our privileged position. Annual model changes are as senseless in styling clothes as in manufacturing automobiles. We do not need big cars or mink coats when the price tag includes less food for the hungry. The demand for cosmetics is based on a cultural definition of beauty. We can just as easily come to see "made up" faces as ugly.

When there is a fertilizer shortage, is it more important to green the grass in cemeteries and suburban lawns, or to fertilize crops for famine areas? On this issue the Synagogue Council of America said, "It should not require great moral courage to insist that the life-sustaining uses of fertilizer take precedence over its ornamental uses."[37] Since feeding grain to cattle produces less food value than if the same grain had been used for human consumption, should we eat less meat? The Overseas Development Council estimates that if each United States citizen ate one less hamburger a week, we could make ten million tons of additional grain available for the hungry of the world. It has also been estimated that the grain used for one year's consumption of alcoholic beverages in the United States would feed almost twenty million persons in India. Is this a new argument for abstinence during the cocktail hour?

Research students at the University of Arizona, instead of digging into waste piles of past civilizations in the Middle East, undertook a modern archeological examination of garbage cans in Tucson. They found that the average household wastes about 9 percent of its food—and this does not include what goes down the garbage disposal![38] Were T. S. Eliot now rewriting his description of our wasteland, he might add to "a thousand lost golf balls" dozens of half-eaten steaks left on restaurant and patio tables.

Do we not need to restate our aspirations about material standards of living? At what point do we thoughtlessly succumb to a contemporary infatuation with decadence? Should we update the model of family consumption which we present to our children? The reasons for this are especially compelling for Christians. In view of the biblical em-

Chart 4
COMPARISON OF U.S. OFFICIAL DEVELOPMENT ASSISTANCE AND SELECTED U.S. PERSONAL CONSUMPTION EXPENDITURES, 1973 ($ BILLIONS)

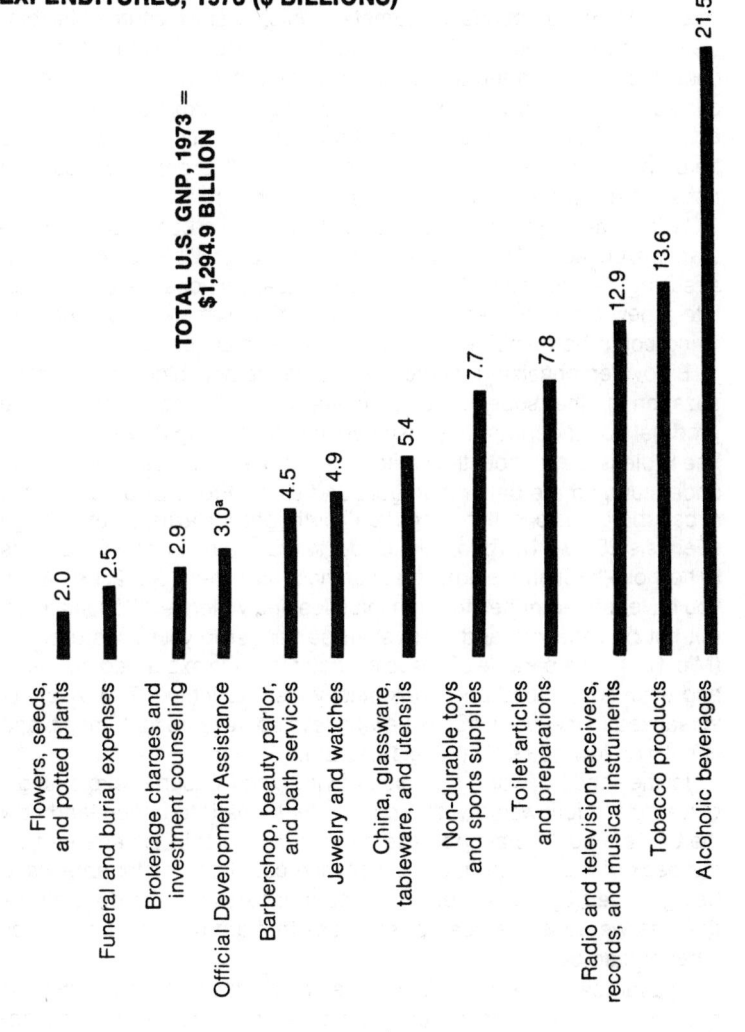

TOTAL U.S. GNP, 1973 = $1,294.9 BILLION

Category	$ Billions
Flowers, seeds, and potted plants	2.0
Funeral and burial expenses	2.5
Brokerage charges and investment counseling	2.9
Official Development Assistance	3.0[a]
Barbershop, beauty parlor, and bath services	4.5
Jewelry and watches	4.9
China, glassware, tableware, and utensils	5.4
Non-durable toys and sports supplies	7.7
Toilet articles and preparations	7.8
Radio and television receivers, records, and musical instruments	12.9
Tobacco products	13.6
Alcoholic beverages	21.5

[a]Net disbursements.
SOURCE: Overseas Development Council, *Agenda for Action, 1975,* p. 259.

phases summarized in the latter part of Chapter 1, we of all persons should be acutely aware of the obligation of stewardship of whatever wealth we have. From a Christian perspective property does not exist for the pleasure of the owner but for the welfare of humankind.[39] Instead of the conspicuous consumption which is still a source of social status, conscientious Christians would be conspicuous for their non-consumption of numerous items. In spite of the second chapter of James (2:1-17) many congregations by their common usage still encourage the custom of costly apparel worn to church. This practice helps publicize the image of the church as a hoarder or protector of riches in a world of squalor and rising resentments.

With fewer physical things we could enjoy life considerably more than we do now. As was briefly pointed out in Chapter 4, by now stressing the provision of social and spiritual services, we could enter into a new era of human history. A reduction in material standard of living could be combined with a rise in the total standard of living.

By overemphasizing inferior values we are now blocking the actualization of other superior values in life. We are in the situation of the prodigal squandering our substance in riotous living (Luke 15:11-32). The Bible is clear about the limitations of material goods. Wisdom and understanding are better than gold and silver (Proverbs 3:13-14). It is a bad bargain to sell our spiritual birthright for a mess of pottage (Genesis 25:29-34). To forsake God, "the fountain of living waters," is to hew out "broken cisterns, that can hold no water" (Jer. 2:13). When you have reaped riches through injustice and violence, "You shall eat, but not be satisfied, and there shall be hunger in your inward parts" (Mic. 6:14). In a parable of Jesus the rich man who expanded his barns and enjoyed his food and drink, finally lost everything. This was universalized in the word, "So is he who lays up treasure for himself, and is not rich toward God" (Luke 12:16-21).

In the modern world "gracious living" can become exploitation, blocking full fellowship with God. We find it hard to understand how the captain could claim to have meaningful worship experiences on the deck of a slave ship, or how anyone could be comfortable while being served by the slaves. We should understand. We do it all the time, as we consume scarce resources that are urgently needed by other human beings.

In a radical break with the past we could stress activities which do not exploit persons or the environment—simple recreation, the appreciation of nature or of art and music, reading and education, worship and private devotions, personal and interpersonal growth groups, social action for important reforms. What would happen if we advertised such valuable nonmaterial services as effectively as we have publicized material luxuries? The abundant life can be found best in loving, praying, and contributing to supportive communities. In the light of that fact it is understandable that a British traveler should have said of New York City, "It is the most underdeveloped place I ever saw."

The great religions of mankind have agreed that death comes from rapacity, greed, pride, and materialism, and that life is to be found through moderation, compassion, and enlightenment. According to recent ecological findings, the planet itself underscores this message. Indispensable now is not only discipline in the use of material resources, but imagination in the expansion of nonmaterial resources. In the words of Isaiah, "Then shall your light break forth like the dawn, and your healing shall spring up speedily"(58:8).

ACCENT ON ACTIVISM

Not only is our use of money to be redirected, but also our investment of energy. Any lifestyle to be acceptable for the Christian must move beyond both destructive behavior and apathetic idleness. A distinctive characteristic of the authentic Christian is active intervention to improve established institutions and practices. Subversive *in*activity can have as serious consequences as subversive activity. According to Jesus, it is not enough worshipfully to enunciate, "Lord, Lord" (Matt. 7:15-27). We are known by our fruits in *doing* the will of God in the many roles in which we find ourselves.

Church persons have a thousand faces. We are lawyers, parents, neighbors, county residents, farmers, national voters, department store customers, homemakers, business executives, coal miners, Parent Teacher Association members. Through its laity the church pervasively penetrates the complex structures of society. Sizable religious groups are not helpless before the power structures that make the major decisions. The church has members, who could become vocal representatives, scattered throughout the structures of power all the way from the top elite to grass roots groupings.

With respect to the economic and political issues we have been discussing, each of us normally plays three major roles—as worker, consumer, and citizen. At work we have varying amounts of influence on the policies of corporations, labor unions, or professional associations. The personnel manager of a large company can do more about fair employment practices than can the typical church convention. A worker in a union leadership position can influence strike demands in relation to the total economy, or even have some influence on the foreign policy statements of labor meetings. Each consumer faces the standard of living question previously discussed. Religiously motivated buyers will select brands of items with one eye on price and quality, and the other eye on the social policies of the supplier. We can use the influence of purchasing power, for example, in withdrawing patronage from anyone refusing to bargain with a legitimate labor union, or in supporting anyone who had made a special effort toward pollution control. As citizens we have all the privileges provided by a democracy for participating in local community decisions, and in state and national politics.

In our various roles we can develop uncommon competence in caring, greater effectiveness in service. No one of us can work at everything that needs to be done. But all of us can choose one or a few personal points for concentration. Using four criteria for choice, we might well specialize in those problem areas that are (1) most basic, (2) most urgent, (3) most neglected, and (4) best suited to our particular backgrounds and abilities. For working on our selected issues we can perfect our skills in several important types of activity, such as the following.

1. Develop the art of creative conversation. Public opinion is still, to a great extent, formed by face-to-face verbalization, or "mouth-to-ear resuscitation." While expensive publicity plays a heavy part, personal contacts have important psychological advantages. People can change people better than the mass media can. Persons on all status levels can become opinion leaders. Well-informed workers in the factory, teachers in the faculty lounge, secretaries in the office can help create new social structures. Without becoming a bore, they can raise the quality of coffee-break or dinner-table conversation. Why should we spend so much time discussing the weather, about which we can do very little, when we could talk about our lifestyle in a hungry world, about which we can do much?

2. Enlarge the range of meaningful correspondence. Conversation can also be put on paper in personal letters. It is important to tell Aunt Susan about the baby's new tooth. It is even more important to the baby's future to share with Aunt Susan your enlightened convictions about tax reform. If your reaction is, "But that just isn't done," you are making the point being discussed in these paragraphs. I am talking about a new lifestyle which is more becoming to the Christian than our customary negligence.

More of the common people should also write to highly influential people. Our pens and typewriters can become amplifiers for our voices in reaching school superintendents, corporation executives, labor leaders, and organization officers. A contribution published in the "Letters to the Editor" column may be more widely read than the newspaper's own editorials. Many economic leaders receive so few communications from the public that a thoughtful letter is read, and several on the same subject make an impression. Members of Congress tabulate letters received, even if they cannot read them all. Between elections we thereby have a voice on such matters as reduction of unemployment or preservation of liberty against extremist threats.

3. Work through organizations. In mass society the average person's strength is compounded by joining a group. Realistically speaking, joining one's allies is as essential to social effectiveness in large populations as elevators are a necessity in high rise apartments. Strategic groups may include organizations to which we already belong, such as church school classes or service clubs. Within such groups one may raise issues like our obligation to the disadvantaged and to ourselves—to seek liberation from policies and patterns that enslave us all. One can suggest group programs on issues that are particularly related to the purposes of the organization.

Most of us can give minimal support to more organizations than we have in the past. Even a small contribution, and our name on their membership list, strengthens their purpose. Languishing for support are both local community organizations and national reform groups devoted to such ends as protection of the environment, increase in economic aid appropriations, or support for United Nations agencies. Sending representatives of the church into such well-selected organizations is one version of sending out disciples two by two to carry the gospel.

4. Contribute money to neglected causes. Particularly as families reduce expenditures for material luxuries, they can often greatly increase their giving to organizations working, for example, to increase equality of economic opportunity, or for peace and a reduction of world armament expenditures. In our personal giving we have frequently shortchanged those groups working at the long-range elimination of basic causes rather than at immediate relief of symptoms. In a study of United Church of Christ parishioners, Thomas C. Campbell and Yoshio Fukuyama found that 82 percent made regular contributions to United Funds or Community Chests, while only 10 percent contributed to social reform organizations.[40] Both types of contribution are important, of course; but this percentage of distribution is very

poor stewardship in the kind of world we have been describing in this book. The stubs of one's checkbook still remain one rough measure of Christian citizenship.

5. Volunteer for constructive campaigns. Citizen power must be increasingly mobilized both for short-term efforts like election campaigns, and for long-continued education and action through reform organizations. Our increased leisure is too often squandered in spectator sports instead of dedicated to God's enterprises in rebuilding social structures. Some persons are beginning to take full-time volunteerism seriously as a career. Particularly as families simplify their material requirements, there is not the same need for two full incomes. Either husband or wife can often give up paid employment to do volunteer work in the community—or both husband and wife can secure half-time jobs. As once the desire for women's liberation was expressed in finding a salaried job outside the home, now fulfillment for more husbands and wives is also being found by leaving a former job for service in more important fields that cannot afford to pay a wage.

6. Consider political action a normal part of the Christian life. In facing the need for a new economic order, it has become clear that private philanthropy alone is not enough.[41] Many pressing human needs cannot be met without government initiatives. One of the most important expressions of Christian discipleship is to devote time and energy to changing government policy. We now speak of God's activity in the world as including the establishment of international peace and economic justice and political freedom. None of these is attainable without political action. It becomes as important, then, for a church member to discuss an issue with the mayor or a senator as it is to sing in the choir. It may be more important for the future of humankind to address envelopes in a crucial political campaign than it is to distribute fliers announcing the church bazaar.

The preservation of democracy also requires participation, especially by citizens with the lofty goals of a religious perspective. As I wrote in an earlier book, "After all, politics describes the way in which population-wide decisions are made in a democracy. Either we master the strategy of politics or we lose the values of democracy as a way of life. No one of us would join a demonstration and shout, 'Death to Democracy'—but we do worse. We devote our lives to the realization of that slogan by our political inaction."[42]

Hesitant or self-centered public opinion allows persons without vision to be elected to offices that require unprecedented vision. We have already discussed ways in which our witness might change prevailing opinions. In addition, each of us needs to study emerging issues, support progressive legislation, and vote in every election for those most committed to full freedom and opportunity for all. The "conscience constituency" must refuse to support the nationalists, the racists, and the protectors of unjust privilege, no matter how attractively their programs are packaged by expensive public relations manipulators. No one of us is exempt from these duties of contemporary citizenship.

A considerable number of us are called by God to a deeper involvement in politics. This might mean canvassing the precincts, getting citizens registered and voters to the polls, raising funds, calling on legislators or public officials, or arranging testimony before legislative committees. More of us should become active in the political club or party organization of our choice. Certain kinds of influence can be exerted only from the inside. That is where platforms are written, strategies adopted, and, often, candidates nominated. It is only by painstaking persistence in such a multiplicity of minutiae that great gains for humanity can now be won.

ACTION THROUGH THE CHURCH
In such radical social renovation Christian faith makes the most basic contribution. It transforms our values. Social choice is built on the foundation of an ultimate value system. Thoroughgoing, constructive change can be sustained only by transcendent perspective and supernormal power. All these can be the gifts of a stronger, more authentic church. Building such a church is itself a major contribution to a new earth.

An authentic church, alert to its social mission, will have several characteristics. It will accept its responsibility continuously to educate youth and adults on all the most important social issues, including Christian ethical goals and the social theory underlying specific policies. Since the finest economic and political systems can be contaminated by immoral personnel, an authentic church will continue to facilitate the growth of honest, energetic, altruistic, and socially responsible citizens. In its own actions as consumer, employer, and investor the church will set an example for all to emulate. As it challenges its members to less materialistic lifestyles, it will also raise questions about excessive luxury in its own buildings, equipment, and styles of ministry. The church will use more of its budget and staff to influence business and government wherever major moral issues are involved. It will neither be frightened by controversy nor retreat in the face of opposition.

On some of these matters it has been suggested that the church moves with all the deliberate speed of a snail taking a nap. But a renewed church would be transformed by the energizing spirit of God. It would courageously and vigorously lead the most advanced missioners of a new society. Converted members would become new beings in Christ, enthusiastically working as creative nonconformists for unprecedented justice and equal opportunity. That is what it means to be the church. That is what it means to be a follower of Christ. If your congregation were accused of being Christian—of if you were arrested for being a Christian—would there be enough evidence to sustain the charge?

QUESTIONS FOR DISCUSSION
1. What would you add to the list (in the first section of this chapter) of common attitudes in our population that an authentic Christian would reverse?

2. Do you agree with the author that inactivity helps the opposition? What are some of the consequences for our lifestyle as Christians?

3. Mimeograph (or individually construct) a chart listing, in the first column, a variety of consumer items, such as dishwasher, expensive car, cosmetics, liquor or soft drinks, swimming pool, color TV, pets, costly toys for children, diamond engagement rings. Then provide three narrower columns headed "Use as is customary in our society," "Reduce expenditure or use," and "Eliminate entirely." Ask each member of the group to check, after each item, the column which he or she thinks should become his or her own action. Encourage adding and checking additional items. Then discuss reactions in the group.

4. Which are you most honestly dissatisfied about—your lack of certain material items you wish you could have, or your lack of greater spiritual development? In silent meditation, imagine what your life would be like as material consumption was decreased and as social and spiritual development was emphasized. Write down the major insights from your meditation and share with the group. Compare your vision with the Bible. With current television programs.

5. Arrange for a sharing of experiences by those in the group who are working with reform organizations, giving volunteer service to community agencies, or participating in alternate intentional communities. Should others in the group be taking on such assignments?

6. Discuss the appropriateness for Christians of the types of activity discussed in the section on "Accent on Activism." What would you add or subtract?

7. Close the discussion period with a time of private prayer or group worship.

PROJECTS FOR ACTION
1. The text of this chapter includes a great many suggestions for action. Prepare a summary list. Let each individual lift out of the list those he or she resolves to do more about. Those making similar resolutions might covenant and strategize together about next steps. In facing matters such as these, it is always well to ask, "If not you, who? If not now, when?"

2. Again go through the summary list of action items, prioritizing the most important ones to be built into the program of your church, either as direct action by the congregation or as training and support for individual members. Plan and carry through the process for incorporating such program items.

3. Protest to firms whose newspaper ads or television commercials most flagrantly encourage wasteful materialism.

4. Several Christian organizations are suggesting one or more meatless days each week. Adopt such a program for your family.

5. If no such organization already exists, help form a local group to work on world hunger and/or a new economic order. Include churches, but probably also other individuals and organizations.

6. Encourage letters from the members of your congregation on a current issue before Congress. Draw up a fact sheet, give preliminary publicity, and have available in the narthex, after a Sunday service, tables, pens, stationery, and addresses of your representatives in Congress.

7. Develop a telephone network to spread the word whenever letters or telegrams need to go to members of Congress.

SESSION PLANS FOR GROUP USE OF *Good News for Rich and Poor*

by Dieter T. Hessel

A study/action course built around this book should stimulate more than a little reading and conversation on "Christian Approaches to a New Economic Order." *Good News for Rich and Poor* has an ambitious design, keyed to a process of education known as the AAAR cycle. By this is meant a style of learning that encompasses:

AWARENESS
Orientation to issues and apparent action needs; consciousness-raising in a theological context.

REORIENTATION
to the problem and possible action.

REFLECTION
upon the experience, including new values and meanings appropriated by the group.

ACTION
Undertaking specific activity to assist the victims and, with them, to change structures.

ANALYSIS
Probing systemic origins of the problem; thinking strategically about goals and methods

Note that individuals and groups can enter the cycle at any point. Also some settings and groupings are appropriate for portions of the cycle only.

Awareness has several dimensions: (1) awareness of issues in society and the community, in terms of how those issues affect the quality of human life; (2) awareness of God's intention for humankind, expressed in the biblical vision of *shalom,* in Jesus' announcement of the kingdom of God, and in the apostolic message of reconciliation; (3) consciousness of our own responsibility for action in relation to others; and (4) celebration of the active presence of God in the world.

Disciplined analysis of issues must accompany awareness if we are to understand what underlies the problems we face—basic factors, systemic causes—and if we are to formulate meaningful strategies of action. Methods of analysis can include gathering of data, examining one's own experience, simulating systems, and consulting with people who are affected differently by each problem or issue.

Participation in *corporate action* is an essential element of this approach. Action consistent with Christian ethics will vary according to the situation and to the strategic plans of the group. Action should move beyond efforts at service and education to encompass acts of public witness and attempts at structural change.

Reflection is crucial to the learning experience as a follow-up to the action process. There is need for theologically informed reflection on the experience itself, the ethical assumptions, and the motivations on which the action was based. An important result of reflection is an increasing awareness of the issues and the nature of Christian responsibility to meet them. Such reflection enables continuous *reorientation* of learners, both individually and in groups.

This AAAR cycle gives impetus to corporate involvement by Christians who want to impact the behavior of their families, associates, congregations, community institutions, and public officials. Groups of Christians, relating to nonchurch entities as appropriate, are encouraged to plan as a community—i.e., to respond corporately to the issue(s) before them in light of the promise and claims of the gospel. A detailed orientation to this method of Christian education, one of four Shared Approaches being developed jointly by major Protestant denominations, is offered in *Doing the Word: An Interpretive Manual* by Robert E. Koenig (United Church Press), $1.95, available from denominational curriculum order departments.

OPTIONS FOR A STUDY/ACTION COURSE

The simplest way to use this book, within the educational approach just described, is in a six-session course. (To begin properly an introductory meeting of the course group is also necessary, to explain the purpose of the course and to distribute the books—making seven meetings in all.) Participants should read each chapter in advance of the session so that the course group can focus attention on the Questions for Discussion and Projects for Action at the end of the chapter.

Each chapter exemplifies the movement from awareness to

analysis to action, sharpened by continuous reflection. A six-session course may produce little action planning, unless supplemented. Anticipate the need for activity or meetings that parallel and follow up the six sessions of the course group. The intention to follow up with action must be built in procedurally, perhaps by creating a planning group of course participants who gain insight from the six sessions but do not expect the six sessions alone to devise a follow-up program. A subgroup or task force for follow-up planning, which should be legitimated by the governing board of the congregation or congregations from which it is drawn, can work in special meetings that precede and parallel the six-session course, resulting in the presentation to the course group and congregation of a plan of action concerned with a new economic order. This same planning group could take responsibility for introductory mechanics and leadership of the six sessions of the course, using the Questions for Discussion and Projects for Action, and bringing to those sessions some additional information and resources, as suggested in the session plans below.

Fewer than six sessions, plus an introductory meeting, may be required to fit your congregation's calendar or study habits. A shorter course is workable, provided that even more emphasis is given to the creative functioning of an action task force. A five-session course could consider the first three chapters in two sessions, by assigning all of Chapter 1 and the first half of Chapter 2 to Session One, and by assigning the last half of Chapter 2 and all of Chapter 3 to Session Two. A four-session course could involve the same pattern for the first two sessions, with Session Three devoted entirely to Chapter 5, and Session Four taking up both Chapters 4 and 6. *Caution:* do not try to combine Chapters 4 and 5, leaving one meager session for exploration of proposals for change in both domestic and international economic order.

Recognizing that fewer than six sessions may be necessary but is less desirable, the session plans below follow the format of six sessions, preceded by an introductory meeting.

INTRODUCTORY MEETING
After a get-acquainted exercise, give or sell each participant a copy of the book. Highlight the book's purpose and movement as indicated in the table of contents and in the Preface. Explain the educational approach, using the chart of the AAAR cycle, and conclude that explanation with the following overview:

Taken together, the chapters of *Good News for Rich and Poor* move from theological awareness of the need for change (Chapter 1) in the direction of economic health (Chapter 2), over against other existing, but unacceptable models (Chapter 3). Strategic goals and action objectives for a better American economic order are highlighted (in Chapter 4), while special attention is given (in Chapter 5) to policies that lead toward a New International Economic Order. The last chapter (6) relates action opportunities to biblical imperatives, with concrete suggestions for personal and group behavior.

Where it seems appropriate, encourage the course participants to enter into a study/action agreement or "contract" like this one:

I, the undersigned, agree to participate with other members of this congregation for _____ weeks of study/discussion/action concerned with Christian approaches to a new economic order. I agree to read the book *Good News for Rich and Poor* by Harvey Seifert, to participate in meetings of the group dealing with this book, and to share in an appropriate follow-up action that is of mutual interest and that befits the purposes of the church.

I, the undersigned, also agree to plan with other members of this group appropriate follow-up actions, in consultation with the congregation's governing board. This is an extra time commitment.

Date	Name
	Address
	Telephone

If time is available near the close of the introductory meeting, the group could enter directly into discussion question #1, or consider action project #6 at the end of Chapter 1. An interesting alternative would be to show *Glass House,* a striking 12-minute, 16 mm, color film. In this allegory the world is a barren, craggy wilderness in which the poor struggle to salvage what little they can from the worn-out earth. On a tiny patch of grass in the midst of this desolation, one wealthy man luxuriates in his abundance and reads about "world problems" in his newspaper. The film offers an insight into the psychological relationships between the haves and the have-nots. The film may be rented from denominational film distribution centers such as those of the

United Presbyterian Church in the U.S.A.,* or from Mass Media Ministries, 2116 North Charles Street, Baltimore, Md. 21218 (301-727-3270). Rental fee is approximately $15.

SESSION ONE (ADVANCE READING: CHAPTER 1)
This session should focus on the Christian expectation of change. The session might begin with a showing of the 12-minute film, *Glass House* (film information above), if the film was not used at an introductory meeting of the course group.

The first four Questions for Discussion at the end of Chapter 1 make a useful sequence. Question #1 is a form of envisioning. Allow 10 minutes for the group to discuss their hopes for change after dividing into pairs. Each pair can describe the vision of Isaiah 58:6-8 in terms of five desirable changes in social and economic life at home and abroad. Anticipate the contrast between new vision and old reality by displaying pertinent news clippings.

To enhance the discussion of Question #3, summarize the six *consequences* of Christian social change, putting each point in a summary sentence. How might your group communicate some of these needed changes to others in the congregation, community, public office?

The procedure for Question #4 should not be rushed; it is an opportunity to list and clarify *criteria for change* on newsprint or posterboard for handy reference in later sessions of the course.

Projects #5 and #6 provide groundwork for analysis of the rich/poor gap and the church's current social ministry. (It may not be feasible to do both projects in the same session. Accurate information on the congregation's current social ministry will need to be obtained by the planning committee between meetings of the course. The main point of this inquiry into congregational activities and spending is to determine how your church relates to the poor. If the criteria for change considered in Question #4 were applied to the congregation's program and budget, what changes would be called for?)

Data pertinent to Action Project #5 are easily obtained from tables published in *The U.S. and World Development: Agenda for Action* (Overseas Development Council, 1717 Massachusetts Ave., N.W., Washington, D.C. 20036; 202-234-8701), $4.50. The chart in Chapter 2 of *Good News for Rich and Poor* is also useful to portray the rich/poor gap.

*Contact your nearest Association Sterling Film Center. For more detailed information on distribution centers, write to: Teleketics, 1229 S. Santee Street, Los Angeles, Calif. 90015.

SESSION TWO (ADVANCE READING: CHAPTER 2)
If Session One is less than two hours long, some of the activities suggested above, especially Projects #5 and #6, may be carried over for consideration in this session. Call attention to the data on the rich/poor gap, supplementing the tables mentioned above with current information from newspapers and magazines. Also look for pertinent data on the growing rich/poor gap in our country (e.g., the average white family has twice as much income as does the average nonwhite family in the U.S.).

Make use of Robert Heilbroner's portrait (p. 25) of the changes that would take place in the life of an American suburban family were it suddenly to become a family in the developing world. Then spend time with Question #1 at the end of Chapter 2. This suggestion to argue *for and against* inequality of income and wealth illustrates an important procedure in social education; viz., change agents should give rational attention to opposing viewpoints rather than jump into a battle of emotions that obscures the search for clarity of moral principle. Question #4 is an important review step to reinforce the analysis of our current economic system offered in Chapter 2. Question #5 brings us back from neutral discourse to examine economic patterns in light of Christian criteria for change.

Project #1 is an excellent tandem activity for Question #1. Project #1 can be carried out in advance of the session by one or more members of the course group who have access to photo files of the local newspaper or are good photographers. Some of the pictures should depict the positive values of center-city life and the negative facets of outlying neighborhoods.

Project #2 has been tried in various ways since people became interested in welfare reform. One approach is described in *The Christian Century,* January 22, 1975, pp. 60ff, "A Hunger Exercise," by Richard A. Hoehn.

Regarding Project #3, consult your denominational hunger office for advice on simulation meals, and liturgical and discussion resources.

SESSION THREE (ADVANCE READING: CHAPTER 3)
Reproduce on newsprint the "horseshoe" chart that appears in Chapter 3, and review the author's explanation of its categories. Note that communism is a prominent example of totalitarianism on the Left, while fascism exemplifies totalitarianism on the Right. Then ask, as in Question #3, "Which general position on the 'horseshoe' chart do you consider most desirable to meet social justice demands?"

Invite participants to suggest some economic policy implications of their choice, but do not allow participants to criticize each other's views. In fact, the more pluralism of preferences, the more interesting this session ought to be. The most likely outcome, however, is a clustering of preferences for moderate conservatism and moderate liberalism.

Moderation on questions of economic justice is not necessarily best. Is gradualism in either direction adequate to meet the challenges of social and economic change? Seifert has argued in another of his books, *Ethical Resources for Political and Economic Decision* (Westminster Press, 1972), p. 131, that gradualism may be a form of benign neglect. "Those who practice this cautious gradualism have too little feeling of dissonance between accepted norm and actual practice.... We become either activists against major evils or accomplices in them." If the goals of economic justice must be achieved more rapidly than they have been to date, what approaches are most valid?

Seifert's review of unacceptable options actually focuses on communism, fascism, *and* economic concentration (oligopoly). In fact, economic concentration may be a bigger threat to justice now than are these others. The group would benefit by additional background information available in the pace-setting book on multinational corporations by Richard Barnet and Ronald Müller, *Global Reach* (Simon and Schuster, 1974).

The process of concentrated and globalized economic power undermines free enterprise, efficiency, equality, and democracy, which are anticipated in our traditional economic philosophy. When the market for any major product (e.g., foods, metals, automobiles, tires, soaps) is controlled by a handful of firms, prices tend to stay artificially high—just opposite of the way the free enterprise system is supposed to work. Efficiency is also decreased by product differentiation (the proliferation of brand names for nearly identical products) and rapid product replacement. Inequality is also aggravated as global companies export production-line jobs to take advantage of cheap labor abroad and to increase profits for shareholders at home—the net result being income redistribution toward the already affluent. As private global economic empires emerge, government has less power to maintain stable employment, to protect the money supply, and to collect revenues. (According to recent issues of the *Economic Report to the President,* corporations in 1958 were contributing more than 25 percent of federal revenues, but by 1973 they were contributing less than 15 percent of federal revenues.)

These figures may seem remote, unless you can identify some local effects of the power of economic conglomerates. One or more plants are likely to be subsidiaries of remote enterprises that could bring pressure to close a plant or to double its capacity, without much accountability to the community either way. By what means can public accountability be enhanced? *Global Reach* has some suggestions. So does the Interfaith Center on Corporate Responsibility, Room 566, 475 Riverside Drive, New York, N.Y. 10027, a project supported by major religious bodies in the U.S. and related to the National Council of Churches.

SESSION FOUR (ADVANCE READING: CHAPTER 4)

"The Contours of a New Order" picks up the threads of Chapter 3 and highlights the need for democratic decision in economic affairs. Question #4 at the end of Chapter 4 invites the group to analyze the arguments for and against the extension of government economic initiatives, and then encourages members of the group to share their own positions. Discussion habits established in earlier sessions of the course will probably determine whether this exchange of views is mind-stretching or merely heat-generating, since "vigorous public debate rages around proposals for additional economic initiatives by democratic government."

Adequate time should be allotted to carry out the procedure Seifert recommends in the section of Chapter 4 headed, "Areas for Government Action." Question #5 refers to the same procedure. Note that the issue is not whether to have government intervention, but what kind. What kind of economic planning should government do, and with whom, in order to "promote the general welfare"? Seifert offers a more detailed analysis of the economic planning task in *Ethical Resources for Political and Economic Decision,* Chapter IV, "Directions for Decision."

At this point in the course it would be helpful to hear a preliminary report from the follow-up planning committee regarding possible action projects pertaining to economic democracy that may be implemented by the group. Seifert's own list of projects suggests participation in a co-op, design of a workshop, or advocacy of public policy changes. The group should indicate how interested it is in the proposed project(s), so that the planning committee can proceed more effectively.

SESSION FIVE (ADVANCE READING: CHAPTER 5)

Focus the group's attention on the realities of the rich/poor gap, using any displays from Session One and referring to the data offered by Seifert in Chapter 5.

"A New Economy for the World" highlights the quest for a New International Economic Order (NIEO). The NIEO is shorthand for new guidelines in international economic relations that would give the developing countries a better share in the resources of a finite world. The present system has resulted in the fact that while the developing countries constitute 70 percent of the world's population, they account for only 30 percent of the world's income. In the words of the Declaration on a New Economic Order, "it has proved impossible to achieve an even and balanced development of the international community under the existing international economic order. The gap between the developed and the developing countries continues to widen in a system which was established at a time when most of the developing countries did not even exist as independent States and which perpetuates inequality." Now the developing countries demand full and equal participation in negotiations over pricing of commodity exports and manufactured imports, access to markets, official aid targets, appropriate aid channels, etc. While these matters have been of concern for over fifteen years, only recently have they received prominent attention in Special Sessions of the United Nations and in related trade conferences. The initial reaction of the United States to the NIEO was highly confrontational; but more recently the U.S. approach, and that of other developed countries, has been conciliatory. Yet very few citizens of developed countries have shown positive interest.

Obtain a current audiovisual that depicts issues of international trade, such as, *World Food: International Trade Barriers,* 8 min., color; rental $10 from the following Film Distribution Centers (600 Grand Ave., Ridgefield, N. J. 07657 / 512 Burlington Ave., La Grange, Ill. 60525 / 6644 Sierra Lane, Dublin, Calif. 94566); or rental $12.50 from Mass Media Ministries (see p. 88 for address). This brief film shows how developed nations can force developing nations into a role of dependency and, in pursuit of trade, can lessen the economic alternatives available to countries that depend on only one or a few products for export. In some cases poorer nations are forced to provide the luxury products of the richer countries in order just to exist. In some countries the result has been at the expense of developing crops for internal use in feeding the hungry. Film message: Food aid is a stopgap measure, a holding operation until poor countries can grow more food and the international deck of trading cards can be shuffled and redealt.

At this point, the issues of the NIEO can be further clarified by acting out the role play suggested in Question #4 at the end of Chapter 5. Questions #5 and #6 follow naturally, as do Projects #4 and #5.

Seifert observes in Project #3 that "Churches have engaged in economic assistance for a long time." Ask your denominational headquarters for some examples of development projects that might receive special educational attention and financial support in your congregation. Be sure to ask for available resources for intergenerational use (with children and youth along with adults) in worship or social gatherings of the church.

Appended is a litany that was first produced by a consortium of denominations working on bread-and-justice issues under the acronym of WHEAT (World Hunger Education and Action Together), Room 634, 475 Riverside Drive, New York, N.Y. 10027. WHEAT also offers free copies of a five-point covenant wherein church members commit themselves to:
   a. Intensive study of root causes in Christian theological perspective;
   b. Direct involvement in local hunger issues;
   c. Advocacy of public policy changes through existing networks such as BREAD FOR THE WORLD and IMPACT;
   d. Financial support for denominational development programs;
   e. Change of individual/family/institutional lifestyle.

SESSION SIX (ADVANCE READING: CHAPTER 6)

The Christian lifestyle change portrayed in this chapter makes exciting reading. The Questions for Discussion and Projects for Action at the end of Chapter 6 offer excellent advice for getting started. Note that lifestyle change should be oriented not only to individuals but also to families and institutions (including whole congregations). Significant changes require continuous support because they clash with consumerism. Consumerism is, in some respects, like drug addiction. Breaking the habit is almost impossible without support groups.

The first support group must be the people with whom we live. Families are the basic economic units of society, and most of our consumption is done in the context of these units. Get the whole family to be a mutual support group, experimenting with reduced and more efficient consumption of food and energy resources. Include the children.

Congregations have also formed support groups. The families meet together periodically to discuss the kinds of things they are experimenting with and to share their successes and failures. These groups in local congregations can look at their church's consumption patterns as well as those of their families.

There is a danger in forming support groups solely for the purpose of working on reducing consumption. Reduced consumption is not an end in itself; it should be sought in the larger context of dealing with bread-and-justice issues through study, political action, direct involvement, and financial support.

Among the agencies that offer practical models for creative simplicity are:

Alternatives, 1924 E. Third St., Bloomington, Ind. 47401, which publishes a 16-page quarterly newsletter available for $5 annually.

Mennonite Central Committee, 21 S. 12th St., Akron, Pa. 17501, which offers an excellent cookbook (available from Herald Press, Scottdale, Pa. 15683, $4.95) and related bibliographical suggestions.

Shakertown Pledge Group, 4719 Cedar Ave., Philadelphia, Pa. 19143, which features an 8-page pledge available at 10 for $1.

Simple Living Program (of the American Friends Service Committee), 2160 Lake St., San Francisco, Calif. 94121, which has produced an excellent booklet entitled *Taking Charge,* available for $1.

A HUNGER LITANY IN THREE "LANGUAGES"

(The litany reflects the fact that there are various approaches to the analysis of poverty, its causes and solutions worldwide. Each approach expresses truth. For most persons there is a progression from the first to the second to the third analysis [A, B, C]. The analysis applies within a country as well as internationally.)

Liturgist A: Lord, the Good News impels us to share food with the hungry.

Congregation: We are grateful that you have given us communication and transport and resources so that the thrust of famine may be lessened.

Liturgist B: Yet, our hearts are troubled.

Congregation: We realize now that the problems of hungry people will press in on us the rest of our days.

Liturgist C: Third and Fourth Worlds cry out despite our offerings.*

Congregation: Some even say hunger is not the issue. Help us to understand.

---

*The "First World" is considered to be the industrialized nations of the non-socialist world: USA and Canada, Western Europe, Japan, Australia, etc. The "Second World" is composed of the socialist countries: Russia, Eastern Europe, China. Until recently, "Third World" meant all the developing countries not under either of the first two umbrellas. Some of them today are faced with such poverty (e.g. Bangladesh, sub-Saharan Africa, parts of Latin America) that they are being called the "Fourth World."

Liturgist A: Of course hunger is the issue. You can see it in the famine-stricken ... the children with swollen stomachs, the listless eyes, the despairing silence in the face of starvation. What they need is food, good simple food.

B: There's truth to what you say, but there's more to be said. The real need is for development. Hungry people must be enabled to develop their own resources, including food production, especially that.

C: The issue goes far beyond what either of you is saying. The problem is exploitation. We must rearrange world economics so that resources are distributed with more equity. Then all would be able to have the food they need. Those who can buy never go hungry.

Congregation: Lord, the times are bewildering. We'd rather turn our face away and pretend no problem exists. Nevertheless, give us translating hearts so that we may see the shapes of the question in many languages.

A: You've seen the massive food airlifts. It's a great story in the Christian tradition of charity.

B: But people will starve anew if they aren't taught to help themselves. Not food but technical aid and example must be our assistance.

C: We still buy their raw materials cheap and sell finished products back at high price. And two billions must live on $200 a year. Justice is required.

A: If people are dying of hunger you give them a fish.

B: If people are to live tomorrow you help them learn to fish.

C: I say make room at the stream so that everyone *can* fish... and make a market where people who fish can sell their surplus catch.

Congregation: Lord, give us a new sense of community and a sense of being neighbors to people all over the world. We are proud to be Americans. Let not our pride prevent us from caring for others of the human family.

A: It is the story of being a Good Samaritan.

B: Even more it is the story of the talents and giving poor nations the chance to develop two talents into ten.

C: Mary sang it in the Magnificat: He has put down the mighty from their seats and exalted them of low degree. He has filled the hungry with good things and the rich are sent empty away.

Congregation: Lord, is it possible we are to receive as well as to give? Can the world's poor give us new visions of how humanity should live? Do they have a mission to us as well?

A: We can give of our surplus—money, food, clothing.

B: We can give of our know-how, our technology, our organizing ability.

C: But the poor claim more—the right to have enough for life. We can let the system be changed so that all get a share of the earth—which God owns.

A: We regret the dependency, but a dying man is willing to be dependent.

B: Self-reliance is the word.

C: We need a shift of power and wealth in an unbalanced world.

Congregation: Lord, help us to learn the languages and to know the directions. Which side must we take? Where do you stand, Lord?

A: Immediate relief aid for the starving.

B: Assistance for self-help.

C: Internal reform, international economic change, or in desperation, overthrow.

Congregation: Lord, what shall we do?

A: We haven't begun to give what is needed.

B: We must support agriculturists, technicians, rural development projects.

C: We need to lobby in Congress to change our policies of aid and trade.

Congregation: God of the hungry and of the full,
God of the poor and of the rich,
you have spoken a strong word,
a beautiful and terrible word
of liberation and salvation, of freedom and unity,
to all your children, through Jesus, in the Spirit's power.
May your Spirit move us to stop resisting,
so that we may really will to live
and exercise the freedom you have given us:
freedom from our selfishness and our possessiveness,
freedom from our idols and property and plenty,

freedom from our worship of a social order
in which others starve while we have our fill.
Teach us to take our lives and our institutions in hand,
making them serve you through serving our neighbors,
reshaping them for worldwide sharing.
We pray clearly and surely in Jesus' name. Amen.

NOTES

1. *Fellowship,* March, 1974, p. 11.
2. *Newsweek,* September 15, 1975, p 37.
3. Loc. cit.
4. Rubem Alves, *Tomorrow's Child* (Harper & Row, 1972), p. 196.
5. Helmut Gollwitzer, *Rich Christian and Poor Lazarus* (Macmillan 1970), pp. 88-89.
6. Gustavo Gutierrez, *A Theology of Liberation* (Orbis, 1972), p. 276.
7. Harvey Seifert, *Ethical Resources for Political and Economic Decision* (Westminster Press, 1972), p. 47.
8. Kenneth E. Boulding, *The Meaning of the Twentieth Century* (Harper & Row, 1964), p. 7.
9. Herman P. Miller, *Rich Man, Poor Man* (Thomas Y. Crowell Co., 1971), p. 157. Herman P. Miller, "Inequality, Poverty, and Taxes," *Dissent,* Winter, 1975. Cf. Lester C. Thurow, *Generating Inequality* (Basic Books, Inc. 1975), Chapter 1.
10. Benjamin Okner, "Middle Class Tax Reform?" *transaction,* March-April, 1971, p. 60.
11. Henry B. Clark, *Escape from the Money Trap* (Judson Press, 1973), Chapter 5.
12. Robert L. Heilbroner, *The Great Ascent* (Harper & Row, 1963), pp. 23ff.
13. Arthur Simon, *Bread for the World* (Paulist Press, and Wm. B. Eerdmans Publishing Co., 1975), p. 45.
14. Lester B. Pearson, "Trade, Aid, and Peace," *Saturday Review,* February 22, 1969, p. 26.
15. Louis Turner, *Invisible Empires: Multinational Companies and the Modern World* (Harcourt Brace Jovanovich, 1971), pp. 135-36.
16. John K. Galbraith, *American Capitalism* (Houghton Mifflin Company, 1956, 2d edition, revised), p. 91.
17. Richard Lichtman, *Toward Community: A Criticism of Contemporary Capitalism* (an occasional paper of the Center for the Study of Democratic Institutions, 1966), p. 17.

18. Richard K. Taylor, *Economics and the Gospel* (United Church Press, 1973), p. 21.
19. *Newsweek,* September 1, 1975, p. 51.
20. Alves, op. cit., p. 26.
21. For additional suggestions see Taylor, op. cit., p. 108, and the Session Plans.
22. Fred J. Cook, *The Nightmare Decade* (Random House, 1971), pp. 148-49.
23. Richard J. Barnet and Ronald E. Müller, *Global Reach: The Power of the Multinational Corporations* (Simon and Schuster, 1974), p. 13.
24. Kenneth E. Boulding, *Beyond Economics* (University of Michigan Press, 1968), p. 47.
25. "The Case for Planning" (The Initiative Committee for National Economic Planning, 901 N. Broadway, White Plains, N.Y. 10603), p. 2.
26. *Newsweek,* September 15, 1975, p. 37.
27. Simon, op. cit., pp. 3-4.
28. Ibid., pp. 4-5.
29. U.S. Arms Control and Disarmament Agency figures, quoted in *Global Justice and Development,* report of the 1974 Aspen Interreligious Consultation (Overseas Development Council, 1975), p. 175.
30. Simon, op. cit., p. 123.
31. Mark O. Hatfield, "World Hunger—the Religious Connection," *Worldview,* October, 1974, p. 53.
32. Address to the American Society of Newspaper Editors, April 16, 1953. Quoted in Simon, op. cit., p. 130.
33. *The Seventh Special Session of the General Assembly* (United Nations pamphlet, 1975), p. 3.
34. Ibid., p. 8.
35. Simon, op. cit., p. 103.
36. For a more detailed discussion and supporting evidence, see Barnett and Müller, op. cit., Chapter 7.
37. *Global Justice and Development,* op. cit., p. 112.
38. Arch Napier, "Garbage Archaeology," *Human Behavior,* July, 1975, pp. 59-60.
39. For more complete discussion of the ethics of property, see Harvey Seifert, *Ethical Resources for Political and Economic Decision* (Westminster Press, 1972), pp. 55-63.
40. Thomas C. Campbell and Yoshio Fukuyama, *The Fragmented Layman* (United Church Press, 1970), p. 57.

41. For a broader discussion of general political strategy, see Seifert, op. cit., pp. 121-42.
42. Harvey Seifert, *Power Where the Action Is* (Westminster Press, 1968), p. 99.

ADDITIONAL READING

Resolutions from the Sixth and Seventh Special Sessions of the United Nations on the NIEO are obtainable free of charge from the Office of Public Information, United Nations, New York, N.Y. 10017.

Cowap, Chris, *Where's Your Treasure? Where's Your Heart?* Church Women United, 1975. Obtainable from P.O. Box 134, Manhattanville Station, New York, N.Y. 10027 at 25¢ each, or 12 for $2. Ms. Cowap examines the monetary aspects of human development. It is easily readable and relates most appropriately to the U.S. situation.

Dickinson, Richard D. N., *To Set at Liberty the Oppressed: Towards an Understanding of Christian Responsibility for Development/Liberation*, Geneva, 1975: World Council of Churches. This is the follow-up on *Line and Plummet* and brings together once more the best minds of WCC's Commission on the Churches' Participation in Development. It continues to study the ethos of development with on-target suggestions for the church. Available at $5 from WCC, Room 439, 475 Riverside Dr., New York, N.Y. 10027.

Elliott, Charles, *Patterns of Poverty in the Third World,* New York, 1975: Praeger. Here the author of *Development Debate* considers in meticulous detail certain theories about the causes of hunger, under-development, underemployment, etc. This is a "meaty" book with much data, but written in lucid style. Available from WCC, Room 439, 475 Riverside Dr., New York, N.Y. 10027, $6.95.

Gardner, Richard N., *New Structures for Economic Interdependence,* Institute of Man and Science, Rensselaerville, New York, 1975. In this publication, the well-known professor from Columbia University reports on and analyzes a consultation meeting of internationally known experts before the opening of the Seventh Special Session of the United Nations. Good background material for the implications of NIEO. Available from Institute of Man and Science, Rensselaerville, N.Y. 12147, $2.

Gatt-Fly, *What Is the New International Order?*, 1975. This is a Canadian view of the trade and tariff aspects of NIEO. It distinguishes itself in its most readable yet informative style. Available free from Gatt-Fly, 600 Jarvis St., Toronto, Ontario M4Y 2J6, Canada.

Haq, M., "New Structures for Economic Independence," May, 1975, and "A New Framework for International Resource Transfers," June, 1975. Both papers are excellent and relevant studies by this distinguished economist at the World Bank. Available from the Aspen Institute, Aspen, Colo. 81611.

"The Third World Forum: Intellectual Self-Reliance," *International Development Review,* November 1, 1975. The article deals with the reasons for the establishment of the Third World Forum, which consists of the most distinguished development economists from Asia, Africa, and South America. The Forum was called together in Karachi, Pakistan, in 1975 and seeks to amplify the voice of indigenous ideas. M. Haq believes that the Forum will become the dominant intellectual and political force of the next decade.

"The New International Economic Order and the Churches," WCC. A response from this top ecumenical body. Available from WCC/CCPD, 150 route de Ferney, 1211 Geneva 20, Switzerland.

INTERCOM #78. This is an excellent guide to discussion, study, and resources on the issues of global interdependence. It contains impressive text graphics and up-to-date data on such topics as technology, urban development, natural resources, food, energy, control of the sea, and disarmament. This commendable teaching guide is produced by a joint effort of the Center for War/Peace Studies and the Center for International Programs and Comparative Studies of the New York State Education Department. It is available at $1.75 from INTERCOM, 218 East 18th St., New York, N.Y. 10003.